Eng.d by Geo.E.Perine, New York

REV. JOSEPH LATHROP, D.D.

Born 1731. Died 1820.

Joseph Lathrop

ACCOUNT

OF THE

CENTENNIAL CELEBRATION

OF THE

TOWN OF WEST SPRINGFIELD, MASS.,

Wednesday, March 25th, 1874,

WITH THE

HISTORICAL ADDRESS OF

THOMAS E. VERMILYE, D. D., LL.D.,

THE POEM OF MRS. ELLEN P. CHAMPION,

AND OTHER FACTS AND SPEECHES.

Thos. M. Cooley.

COMPILED BY J. N. BAGG.

PUBLISHED BY VOTE OF THE TOWN.
1874.

CLARK W. BRYAN & CO.
PRINTERS
SPRINGFIELD, MASS.

TO THE

CITIZENS OF WEST SPRINGFIELD,

AND ALL THE

CHILDREN AND RELATIVES, NEAR OR REMOTE,

THIS LITTLE

MEMORIAL

IS DEDICATED.

INTRODUCTORY.

A CENTENNIAL ANNIVERSARY is an event in human history too important to pass unnoticed, for very few mortals are privileged to bridge its mighty chasm from shore to shore. Localities depending upon individuals for characterization have, in a lesser degree, the same necessities and the same laws. In both, the scenes are frequently changing, the acts often independent and fragmentary, and the curtain sometimes suddenly falls in the midst of an important action. A century is a great landmark in any local history, and has the same uses to mankind that the guide-board and the mile-stone have to the uncertain traveler.

"Remove not the ancient landmarks which the fathers have set," is the graphic language of inspiration, and it fully accords with the highest human wisdom. This is sufficient evidence that landmarks are needed, and if needed surely they should be heeded.

What better use of a Centennial Anniversary can a township make, than to review its past; to rub off the moss and dusts of time, accumulating on its historic tablets; and by gathering up the scattered wastes of the way, plant new boundaries, and take fresh bearings for its further journey. The present owes to the future its legacies of precious and pleasant memories, its royal deeds, its noble examples of self-denial for the public good, its characters of great men, who, in molding communities have made their names illustrious and their lives sublime, and as far as possible its garnered histories.

West Springfield lays no claim to any exclusiveness in these particulars over her 342 sister town and cityships in the Commonwealth, but as she looks back upon the record of her children, native and adopted, and including the clergy through the vistas of a century, the spirit of the ancient Roman matron infuses her, as pointing backward she proudly exclaims, "These are my jewels." This, then, is our apology, if one is needed, for the memorial following.

THE ANCIENT SCHOOL-HOUSE.

CENTENNIAL EXERCISES.

THE first action of the town, in regard to the Centennial, is embodied in the following article in its annual warrant for town meeting, March, 1873: "To see if the town will take any action in regard to a Centennial Celebration."

At that meeting it was "Voted that J. N. Bagg, Gideon Wells, and Edward Parsons be a Committee to investigate and report what arrangements are necessary for celebrating the Centennial Anniversary of the settlement of the town."

In accordance with their report, in April, 1873, the town voted to raise the sum of $500 to pay such expenses as may occur in the Centennial Celebration, and that Edward Parsons, J. N. Bagg, Julius Day, G. B. Treadwell, Lester Williams, Aaron Bagg, B. W. Colton, Andrew Bartholomew, and Joseph Merrick be a Committee to make arrangements for the celebration.

The Committee had their first meeting January 31, 1874, at the residence of Col. Edward Parsons, who, by reason of ill health, was unable to take an active part in the further preparations and ceremonies. The time of holding the Centennial was there fixed for March 25th, and the result of this and subsequent meetings was the issue of the following Circular of Invitation:

WEST SPRINGFIELD, MASS.

Settled about 1636. Chartered a Parish 1696. Chartered a Town 1774.

The undersigned, a Committee chosen to make arrangements for a Town Centennial Celebration, occurring Wednesday, March 25th, 1874, cordially invite their fellow-citizens, former residents, and all natives of the town, to participate in the public exercises at the new Town Hall, at 10 1-2 o'clock, A. M.

The Historical Address will be by Thos. E. Vermilye, D. D., of New York.

Facts, incidents and anecdotes pertaining to the early history of the town and its families, together with portraits of prominent persons and pastors, solicited.

AARON BAGG,
JOSEPH MERRICK,
J. N. BAGG, } *Committee.*

J. N. BAGG, *Cor. Secretary.*

The following Officers and Committees were also appointed :

President of the Day,

COL. AARON BAGG.

Vice Presidents,

EDWARD PARSONS,
CHARLES ELY,
LESTER WILLIAMS,
JULIUS DAY,
COTTON ELY,
HORACE S. MILLER,
WILLIAM MELCHER,
ANDREW BARTHOLOMEW,
EDWIN H. BALL,
J. C. PARSONS,
JAMES P. ELY,
SAMUEL MORGAN,
JOHN D. SMITH,
RICHARD BEEBE,
NORMAN DAY,
CHARLES A. ASHLEY,
J. L. WORTHY,
GEORGE L. BOWE,
DANIEL PRINCE,
DR. CYRUS BELL,
GEORGE B. TREADWELL.

Marshal,

WILLIAM C. HATCH.

Assistant Marshals,

NORMAN T. SMITH, ETHAN BROOKS.

The Selectmen—Harvey D. Bagg, Henry A. Sibley and Amos Russell—not only acted as Committee on Finance, but performed various other services where help seemed necessary.

COMMITTEE ON MUSIC.—Joseph Merrick, B. W. Colton, Aaron Bagg, Jr., L. F. Mellen, Dr. H. M. Miller, G. C. Buell.

COMMITTEE ON DECORATIONS.—Theo. Belden, Edson Clark, Mrs. Susan A. Bagg, Dea. Samuel Smith, Mrs. D. H. Baldwin, Richard A Bagg, Charles A. Ashley, W. F. Mosely.

COMMITTEE OF RECEPTION.—Aaron Bagg, George B. Treadwell, Julius Day, Andrew Bartholomew, Harvey D. Bagg, Jas. P. Ely,

Lester Williams, H. A. Sibley, Ethan Brooks, Talcott A. Rogers, Samuel Morgan, Benj. D. Ashley, Justin Ashley, Alvin Sibley, D. H. Baldwin, I. B. Lowell, James E. Champion, N. T. Smith, Reuben Brooks.

COMMITTEE ON COLLATION.—Edward Parsons, Julius Day, Andrew Bartholomew, G. B. Treadwell.

The following was a programme of the day:

WEST SPRINGFIELD, MASS.

Settled about 1636. Chartered a Parish 1696. Chartered a Town 1774.

ORDER OF EXERCISES AT THE TOWN CENTENNIAL CELEBRATION, OCCURRING WEDNESDAY, MARCH 25TH, 1874, ON THE COMPLETION OF THE NEW TOWN HALL.

The Exercises began at 10½ o'clock, A. M.

MUSIC BY THE HAYDENVILLE BAND.

1. Voluntary, ... By the Band.
2. Singing, "Home. Sweet Home," . . By the Choirs.
3. Invocation, Rev. E. N. Pomeroy, Pastor of First Church.
4. Scripture Reading, Rev. L. D. Calkins, Pastor of Park St. Church.
5. Singing, "Let children hear the mighty deeds," *Marlow.*
6. Address of Welcome, ... J. N Bagg.
7. Reply, ... Samuel L. Parsons.
8. Poem, ... Mrs. Ellen P. Champion.
9. Music, ... By the Band.
10. Historical Address, Thos. E. Vermilye, D. D., LL.D, of New York.
11. Singing, "Shall old acquaintance be forgot?" *Auld Lang Syne.*
12. Prayer, . Ashbel G. Vermilye, D. D., of Schenectady, N. Y.
13. Doxology, "Praise God from whom all blessings flow," *Old Hundred.*
14. Benediction, ... Dr. T. E. Vermilye.

The following description of the day and assemblage, is from one of the neighboring journals:

West Springfield's Centennial was as perfect as an event ought to be which can occur but once in a hundred years; as excellent in its own way as the generous bloom of the aloe, shining in the midst of stormy March, amid its forbidding lance-leaves, and induing the century gone and that begun with a fragrant memory. The winds themselves were charmed to mildness, yesterday, and breathed from the south to mark the welcome of the occasion. And heartily was that welcome responded to. The old Common was bordered with waiting horses and vehicles, by the hour of opening, and the handsome hall of the new town-house was filled with as fine looking an assemblage as any old town could gather; many venerable men and women were there, and the active citizens of to-day seemed not unworthy to wear the honors of their predecessors, whose portraits, in quaint attire and with a queer family resemblance in their very varied countenances, looked approvingly upon them. The platform was occupied by a distinguished array of men of hoary heads, with now and then an exception, chief among these being our Asiatic townsman, Mr. Laisun.

The new Hall was tastefully festooned and decorated, and from its walls were suspended the following portraits of its former citizens: Rev. John Woodbridge the first minister of 1698, Rev. Joseph Lathrop D. D. the third minister of 1756, Rev. John M. Chapin the twelfth minister of 1872, Justin Ely 1st, and his wife Ruth White of 1739, Justin Ely 2nd, and his wife Lucy Barron of 1772, Heman Ely, Theodore Ely, Theodore W. Ely, Miner Stebbins, Mrs. Sibyl Taylor Bagg, Sewall White, Dr. Reuben Champion, Heman Day, Aaron Ashley, Daniel Ashley, Hosea Bliss, Rev. D. T. Bagg, Hon Samuel Lathrop, Capt. Henry Phelon, and Hosea Day.

The band prefaced the celebrative exercises with the imposing strains of Keller's American hymn, and then came the simple melody of "Home, Sweet Home!" sung by the united village choirs. The Invocation by Rev. E. N. Pomeroy, is here given, because it was the first public prayer offered in the new Town Hall, and is in part dedicatory.

INVOCATION.

O thou most high and mighty One, who art from everlasting to everlasting; who dwellest in immensity; who hast created this wide universe from nothing; who hast created us from the dust of the earth, and hast breathed into our nostrils the breath of thine own life that we have become living souls. O thou before whom angels bow and archangels veil their faces, we come before thee now in reverence and humility, and begin these exercises with prayer to thee.

We thank thee for life, the great boon of existence which having once given thou dost never recall; we thank thee that we live in this favored land; we thank thee for all the social, educational, political and religious privileges that we enjoy; we thank thee that we are permitted to be here to-day; we thank thee for this spacious building in which we are assembled.

May we remember that much will be required of them to whom much is given; may we make a right use of the various gifts of thy kindness; may we make a proper use of this noble edifice; may we transmit unimpaired to coming generations the civil and religious liberties, privileges and institutions, which by thy gracious kindness and by the self-sacrificing efforts of our fathers, have been intrusted and transmitted to us.

Be thou with us on this interesting and important occasion. Assist all who shall take part in these exercises. Especially be with thy servant, a former pastor of one of these churches, who is to address us to-day; and be with all who in time to come shall occupy the positions that we now hold, when the places that now know us shall know us no more forever. Ever may thy word be preached here in its purity. Ever may truth and righteousness prevail here. Ever may civil and religious liberty be enjoyed here; and may we ever show ourselves to be indeed a people whose God is the Lord. In the name of Christ. Amen.

The Rev. L. D. Calkins then read portions of the 90th and 105th Psalms, beginning with, "Lord, thou hast been our dwelling place in all generations," and was the first Scripture publicly read in the building, after which the old hymn," Let children hear the mighty deeds," was sung with excellent spirit and effect.

The addresses and poem follow in the order of delivery.

THE WELCOME BY MR. J. N. BAGG.

MR. PRESIDENT, LADIES AND GENTLEMEN:—A little more than a year ago, some persons turning over the public records, made the discovery that the town was nearing its centennial birthday. It was thought that the event was of sufficient importance to warrant a celebration. The objects contemplated by such a ceremony, were the preservation of loose local histories and the cultivation of a becoming reverence for the past and high-toned principle among children and those who are now in active life. Accordingly, on the recommendation of one of our citizens, the town, in April last, appointed a committee of nine to carry out the spirit of this service in which we are about to engage. This, briefly, is the origin of the Centennial Celebration. The time was fixed, March 25th, because that was about the time of the first town meeting. The town was incorporated in February, 1774; the first town warrant was issued March 14th; the first town meeting was held March 23d. A circular was issued about the 1st of February, inviting the former residents and others of the town to participate in this exercise that brings us to the end of the century.

Col. Benjamin Day was the first moderator, the first selectman and the first representative West Springfield ever had, and, considering that he was only 32 years old, I think you will agree with me that he must have been a large pattern of a man. He died in 1808, at the age of 97. His descendants remain with us still, and the portrait of his son Heman, who died in 1837, at the age of 82, adorns yonder wall. That Heman was the man who, in his 21st year, in 1776, shouldered the big elm in Shad Lane, whose circumference to-day is 24½ feet, and planted it there. That elm is one of the largest in the State, and for the last 50 years its size and symmetry have been the admiration of thousands. The characteristics of Heman Day and his neighbors are shown in the following squib of his time:

"What time o'dee?" says Walter Cooley;
"Eleven o'clock," says Judah Bagg;
"Time to repent," says Parson Lathrop;
"Time enough yet," says Heman Day.

The Day blood, like that of the world-renowned Morgan horse, both of which are partly indigenous to West Springfield, is strong stuff, and has a good deal of iron in it yet. But I leave history to an abler head and hand.

We stand, to-day, on the crest of a century. I am deeply impressed with the rarity of the occasion and the solemnity of the hour. We shall never participate in a second centennial service. We are making history, and our own acts link us to the ages. Faith, reverence, good will to man are the emotions becoming us now. We are gathered within these new walls to dedicate them by this service, to God and mankind. This new building fitly represents our new century life. Long may it stand to commemorate this occasion, and may the uses of education and political liberty, which its founders had in mind in its erection, ever find here a congenial home.

My friends, in the name and behalf of my fellow citizens, and the committee of arrangements, I have been authorized to extend to you all the hand of greeting and the voice of welcome. Let us bear in mind that this is West Springfield's natal day, and that she desires to commemorate the event by this birthday party. All centenarians, by virtue of their age, are entitled to reverence and filial honor. Fathers, mothers, brothers, sisters! we are made glad by your presence, to-day. Your return is an evidence that you have not forgotten the old roof-tree, and that the altar fires of home still burn in your hearts. We felt that we should have been recreant to every fraternal sentiment if we did not beckon you to the old homestead and make ready the fatted calf because you are returned safe and sound. I bid you welcome, thrice welcome, to our home and yours.

If I were to particularize, I should address the natives who, after years of absence, find themselves strangers in the place of their birth. Some of you went out single-handed and, like Jacob, come back two bands. We welcome also the natives by marriage rite—those who would have been born here if they could, and are not to blame for what they couldn't help! You are the real husband—men and women of the earth. We rejoice that you are guided by silken bonds. We are proud of you for your tractability. We welcome, also, those who lay claim to us by remote ancestry, the children who rejoice in the prefix of great. We welcome those whom the attractions of pleasure and business have brought among us. To the absent friends, remembered and beloved, with us in spirit, we send hearty greetings.

And now, one and all, welcome, doubly welcome, "The heart feels most when the lips move not." We welcome you to the homes of your childhood, to the altars of your God, to the graves of your kindred. As you meet and recognize each other, may the sentiments of honor and principle dignify and ennoble you. Grand old West Springfield, may you ever be the joy and pride of your sons and daughters!

THE REPLY BY MR. SAMUEL L. PARSONS.

MR. PRESIDENT, FRIENDS AND FELLOW CITIZENS:—In the name and on behalf of the natives and former residents of West Springfield, I tender you our most hearty thanks for your kind invitation to return and unite with you in commemorating the one hundredth anniversary of the incorporation of the town. The beautiful address of welcome just pronounced is cheering evidence that you still consider that we have some rights here that you feel bound to respect, and although we may have formally transferred our titles to other hands, yet our very souls still yearn after the flesh-pots of other days. While we may have found delights in other fields, still the sweets of the old pasture have as yet found no rivals.

From twenty to forty years ago, we transferred to your care, in trust, the interests of this, our beloved home, and there are numerous questions that naturally enough rise in the minds of these returning pilgrims, in regard to the use that has been made of these trusts; a few of these questions I wish to propound to you:

First, we left in your keeping a noble, and for this land, ancient town, stretching entirely across the county, kissing the feet of old *Tom*, on the north, and gathering strength as she marched fifteen miles to *grate the Nutmeg* on the south, four very considerable villages, viz.: *West Springfield, Ireland, Agawam* and *Feeding Hills* were her boast. Tell me, do the screams of that noble bird, that so appropriately crowns this beautiful edifice, still call your sons from these extremes? Rumor answers, "No." We are told that *Ireland* has been deprived of her ancient glory by a sad alliance with a fellow who has dared to degrade her by placing upon her neck, a *yoke* with a *Hol* prefixed to it, and who holds her in perpetual bondage.

Agawam and Feeding Hills have likewise acted the part of prodigal sons, and are feeding upon the husks of their own gathering, and so, sir, as we come to look over the ancient pasture grounds, and search for the occupants of other days, we feel a little sad to find the old town shorn of her upper and nether glory, and so many strange flocks feeding in her pastures. Is this, I ask, keeping faith with the once lords of the soil?

We left in your keeping beautiful and wide-spread fields, in this southern vicinity, that you have allowed to be covered over with shops and dwellings, and other evidences of thrift and growth, and have even allowed bands of iron to be stretched across this ancient domain—binding it to the outside world who care little for our comforts or individual rights. Is this, I ask, according to the fathers? We left to your keeping the old Common where unobstructed and free as the air we breathed, we roamed and played at our pleasure; where the general training and cattle-shows were the delights of our youth, and even of our manhood. We return to find that you have aped city notions, and have enclosed these memorable grounds, and have christened it a beautiful Park. Are such things, I ask, in keeping with the notions of former generations?

I have a very joyous recollection of the many very large families, having from eight to twelve children, who occupied these old mansions. I wonder whether there are such families here in these later days. Even down to 1845, the *Massachusetts Gazetteer* said, West Springfield contains 1,030 boys and girls between the ages of four and sixteen years; only thirty-two towns in the State exceeded that number. She also had twenty-five public schools, and 756 voters; how do these figures compare with the facts of to-day?

If, for one moment, I turn your thoughts to a personal matter, I feel quite sure I shall receive your sympathy, for it will come home to other hearts than mine; other large and interesting families have passed through a similar experience. When I look across this beautiful Park for the old house, where the prints of my youthful feet were imbedded in the very floors and stepping stones, and find that old Time and the Vandals have been at work, and my eyes may never again look upon the rooms where in infancy I was rocked to sleep in loving arms; when I call the names of father, mother, and twelve brothers and sisters, and then comes back to me the feeble answer of but one who has maintained the integrity of the old homestead, it seems to me as though the sweets of the time-honored village were largely extracted, and that the power that bound the soul to its early associations is rapidly loosening its grasp. But neither these feet of mine, nor the feet of those who have returned with me to-day have ever forgotten the oft-trodden pathway. Neither from my memory nor from the memories of those who have made the pilgrimage with me, have the experiences of our youth faded away. True, as we enter yonder gathering place of the dead, who were the honored sires and matrons of our childhood, we find more familiar names than we find within these dwellings, and so, in recognizing these facts, we are constrained to admit that changes are taking place—time flies, the enemy of life is busy at his work, the sickle flashes even for us.

I have the faintest recollection of the old church and school-house that stood in the middle of the Common opposite this edifice, but I have a vivid memory of going with my tin pail to gather whortleberries, just east of where the old church stood.

I well remember, sir, how noted West Springfield was for her fat cattle; her farmers were as proud of them as they now are of their bank stocks.

I would not, if I could, forget the happy evenings spent in corn-huskings, apple-parings, and blind-man's-buff, with the adjuncts of cake, cheese, apples and kisses; nor the school-hours, and sleigh-rides—precious memories! Buried realities, for which there is no resurrection!

Some years since there was published a letter from Rev. John Pendleton of Springfield, to Mr. Amos Allen of West Springfield of which the following is a copy:

SPRINGFIELD, July 6, 1787.

MR. AMOS ALLEN:

HONORED SIR:—My kind love to thee and thy wife and dear family, hoping these lines will find you well.

Dear Sir, I know you love to do good, Pray Sir, I intend to cut my grass next Wednesday, if fair; if not, next day, and as we are to make our wants known, if you would be so kind as to let any friends know of the same, and they would come and cut my grass down for me, I hope I should be thankful and obliged to them for the same. Four or five will do it, with what I expect from this side of the river. And pray be so kind the next day after they come and cut my grass, for you and Miss Allen, Deacon Homeston and his wife, Deacon Rogers and his wife, Mr. Lizer and his wife, to come over and see my wife and I, and show me a little to stack my hay, for I am in hopes you and my friends will come and see me oftener than you have done, so then your horses may have some to eat. Dear sir farewell. Yours in love,

JOHN PENDLETON.

But my friends, I have taken enough of your time in dwelling upon the past. As much as we love it, we are prepared to proclaim to the world, that to-day is the best day the world has ever seen. The past century has opened new avenues to the future. We may no longer dwell upon the buried past. New life and activity is being infused into the world; new ideas are to be encouraged; new victories are to be won. Let us buckle on the armor, for the contest before us. At the opening of the century we commemorate, some six million people inhabited this land; to-day forty millions boastfully flaunt the stars and stripes. *Then* we paid tribute to another nation; to-day, after two sanguinary wars, that nation pays tribute to us. *Then* one or two months were necessary to cross the ocean under sails, to the Fatherland. *Now* in 1873, seven hundred magnificent steamers left the port of New York and crossed the ocean, in an average of twelve days. The same steamers brought to these shores 270,000 emigrants to people our lands. In fifteen years, from 1855 to 1869, 2,300,000 emigrants landed in New York.

Then, we used the old tinder-box and flint to light our fires. In 1873, according to the man you love to honor, Mr. Dawes, the government received $2,500,000 revenue, as tax on the lucifer matches made in this country. Then the manufactures of our country were very limited. Now almost every industry of the known world is found within our borders. The first railway in this land was constructed in 1830; thirty miles in the State of Maryland. In 1872, 67,104 miles of railway had been laid, at a cost of $3,159,423,057, and whose earnings in 1872, reached the enormous sum of $472,241,055.

Of these railways, Massachusetts has 1,658 miles, whose earnings in 1872, were $25,363,177.

The letters that pass through our post-offices are almost too numerous to count. The city of New York alone, received in 1873, 16,500,000 foreign letters, and about 45,000,000 domestic letters. Her postmaster is under bonds of $1,200,000 for the faithful performance of his duties. 1,052 clerks and carriers are under his control, and the post-office building now in process of construction in New York will cost more than $7,000,000.

Let us then thank God to-day for this pleasant reunion, and for the advance that has been made in our land during the past century, in manufactures, agriculture, steam-power, labor-saving implements of various sorts, education and the arts, and especially in the developments of a mineral character, gold, silver, iron, copper and lead, which are being discovered as rapidly as there is necessity for them. Neither are the people regardless of morality and religion. Evidences greet us on every hand, that the religious element is very strong in our land, and the foundation of that element is the recognition of one only living and eternal God. But we have also great occasion to rejoice to-day, that not only are there improvements throughout this land and the world, in mechanics, arts and agriculture, but that morality and religion are finding their way into the remotest corners of the earth, and penetrating the islands of the seas. But these matters can only be kept in progress by the hearty and united action of the people. Let us inquire diligently our duty in regard to them, and when the pathway shall be opened to us, be ready to take our place in the foremost ranks and battle for the right, as God may give us strength.

ONLY A STORY.

POEM WRITTEN BY MRS. ELLEN P. CHAMPION OF NEW MARKET, N. H., FOR THE WEST SPRINGFIELD CENTENNIAL.

[READ BY MR. L. F. MELLEN.]

IT is only a story I'm waiting to tell,
Call it vision of sleep, or a wild flight of fancy;
If 'twere conjurer's trick, sooth, he managed it well,
And worked up like magic his shrewd necromancy.

There are spirits so ardent;—no pun, you'll perceive,—
I mean those that go rapping and tipping the table;—
They turn some weak brains, and oft strong minds deceive,
But,—well, here is the mystery, to solve if you're able.

I sat reading last night,—it was lonely and late,
I forget,—it was morning,—yes, midnight and after,
When I heard this strange sound, just outside by my gate,
" Ha, ha, ha," like a burst of the merriest laughter.

In amazement I sprang, half bewildered and dazed,
Then shrunk back, full suspecting some demon of evil;
Were the lights turning blue? No, they cheerily blazed,
"'Tis my rolicking chum," I thought, "home from a revel."

My books suited the hour. One was grewsome; it told
Of fierce, warlike Vikings, a wild dismal story;
My nerves are well strung, but my flesh crept with cold
When the stern pirate heroes walked headless and gory.

Another grim volume, enchanting me quite,
Pictured pale shades in bride robes through dim arches straying,
Where waiting maids, tortured to fainting with fright,
Spent whole nights at their beads, weeping, trembling and praying.

Still my lamp, burning pure, gave me courage and calm,
I e'en smiled at the thought that gaunt ghosts should go stalking;
That strange laugh I had heard, fie! it boded no harm;
'Twas plainly a young moon-struck poet, out walking.

One, the city clocks chimed, pealing near and afar;
Thrice my watchful dog growled; warned, I waited intrusion,
Listening. Loud, louder still, that hobgoblin "ha, ha!"
Dismaying, appalling! A mocking delusion!

'*Tis a witch!* SHE SHALL DIE! If she's *ugly* and *old!*
(That *no* witches exist 'twould be hard to convince us,
But those weird, which disturbed Cotton Mather, I'm told,
Disappeared long ago with their hot pins and pincers.)

The mad shout echoed long. The same voice as before,
Then a foot on the threshold seemed sturdily falling;
That firm step in the hall is no sprite to be sure,
But a bachelor friend, always late, comes a-calling.

The door opened. A stranger, gray, stalwart and tall,
Doffed a queer old cocked hat, bowing slowly and grandly,
"I've dropped in for an hour or two's chat, that is all,
I'm so happy," he said, smiling slyly and blandly.

"You've a sensible fire, friend, birch wood, fragrant, sweet,
Singing songs of the forests while burning and glowing;
That's no back log of tinsel, with fagots to cheat
With their mock flames of gas jets, mere shamming and showing.

"I'm an old-fashioned man. How our lives fly away!
I'm a hundred! You stare,—you wouldn't *suspect* it?
I've made a great feast for my children to-day,
And, ha ha, not a daughter or son shall neglect it.

"'Tis my birthday, you know," looking quizzical still.
"I, a yeoman, was born by this beautiful river,
Though a babe, when the guns boomed at old Bunker Hill,
I shouted, 'tis said, 'Independence forever!'

"My name's Rural, what poets call Sylvan, in rhymes;
My old home such a nook for a bit of day dreaming!

But my sleep is disturbed by the rush of the times,
The whir of swift wheels. and the engine's shrill screaming.

"I'm a wizard,—don't laugh,—this cane is my wand;
Mark through the green meadows those calm waters stealing;
That fair hamlet, broad street, bowered by forest trees grand,
The maple boughs parting, a quaint church revealing."

I thought of Aladdin. The wand waving still.
The scene changed; busy haunts and proud dwellings appearing,
Halls of learning, tall spires, in the vale, on the hill,
And the hum of a city, hard by, I was hearing.

"Now I'll tell you," he said, "just the funniest joke,
Cunning pranks of my children I'm fond of disclosing,
Bold young Holyoke took off half my head, at a stroke,
And Agawam my feet, as I lay one day dozing.

"And,—but this is a secret between you and me;—
Straws show how the wind blows, I have a suspicion
If I'm ever caught napping again, don't you see,
Shad Lane will be gone without asking permission.

"But though robbed of my head, and despoiled of my feet,
Friends declare I've improved,—I don't think they flatter,
For I'm quite sure myself, 'tis a happy conceit,
That each change I have known is a change for the better.

"I'm no dreamer, deploring the past, faded, gone,
Many *Days* still are left me, kind fate is propitious,
And for each *Bliss* that vanished a new *Bliss* is born,"
My guest whispered and winked, he was growing facetious.

"I'm no miser," he said, "though not lacking in pelf,
I've *Baggs* of choice treasure, no coin of it spurious,
But I'm given to prating too much of myself
And family history; I forget you're not curious.

"One word more you will pardon. These doting old eyes
See my children all noble beyond any other;
More faithful, more loyal, more worthy and wise,
Weighed (*Wade) but never found wanting, on sister or brother.

*Hon. Benjamin F. Wade of Ohio, is a native of West Springfield.

"And they coming to-day, I long to behold them;
I'm waiting to greet them with tender caressing;
My fond, empty arms are outstretched to enfold them,
My heart warms to welcome with bounty and blessing."

The voice ceased and the Presence grew formless as air,
The dawn broke gray and chill, with the gusty March weather,
Twilight faded, the lamp dimmed with flicker and flare,
Then guest, warmth, and taper all vanished together.

Hark! is it the south wind that rustles the vines,
Tossing crisp, withered leaves in the wood and the meadow?
Or is it thy voice, O, "long river of pines,"
Whispering low with soft music through mist and through shadow?

Or the bluebird, which seeks her home nest as of old?
Taking Spring now on trust, now in doubt, yet she lingers,
For the elms don their holiday tassels of gold,
And the maples with coral gems deck their brown fingers.

'Tis the bustle and stir in old Ramapoag street,
Sounds of joy and rejoicing disturbing my slumbers,—
I've been dreaming, but this is no charm and no cheat,
This multitude growing with gathering numbers.

'Tis the Century Feast. Swift they come, none are late,—
Some from far northern climes, where too long they've been staying,
Or from warm sunny slopes; from the rich "Golden Gate,"
And from mosques of the East where the Moslems are praying.

All are here, all are here, on this grand natal day,
Their gifts—garnered lore and rare eloquence—bringing,
Tender memories, fraught with the grave and the gay,
Dainty chaplets, sweet minstrelsy, gladness and singing.

All are here; are *all* here? Side by side, dust to dust,
Kindred groups, turf embosomed, in calm silence sleeping,
Theirs the rest which God gives his beloved, through trust,
Till the morning shall come, and the grave yield its keeping.

All are here, all are here! The loved patriot dead,
Names written in stone and remembered in story,

Held safe, safe in our hearts, they who battled and bled
  For their God, for their country, for right and for glory !

And the centuries will pass,—Springs and Autumns told o'er ;
  Still will flow to the ocean our strong, dauntless river ;
Some bluebird will sing in these elms as of yore,
  But each voice of To-Day will be silent forever.

Music followed by the Band,—after which came the great event of the day, *The Historical Address, by Thomas E. Vermilye, D. D., LL.D.*, who more than forty years ago was a Pastor of the First Congregational Church.

W B Sprague,

FOURTH PASTOR OF FIRST CONGREGATIONAL CHURCH.

HISTORICAL ADDRESS.

It seems to be a dictate of nature, to keep alive the remembrance of events of private or social or public interest, by days and acts of formal commemoration. By such means worth is honored, example continues to speak, sentiment exerts its proper control over mere physical motions, and good influences are perpetuated and made permanent. Nothing can be more in accordance on such occasions with the character and spirit of those who settled this country, than the custom handed down from earliest times, to combine religious services with the secular observances. Thus did the Fathers, and thus do we express the conviction that true religion is all-pervading; that God is the guardian both of families and states; that prosperity and safety must rest upon a moral and religious basis; that religion is not so holy a thing as to be placed far apart from the ordinary courses of life, nor the State so weak as to be endangered, or lose its proper position by such contact; that neither the purity of the one, nor the independence of the other, is necessarily impaired or jeoparded by such a union of Church and State. No country has, in reality, been kept more free from entangling alliances of this kind, yet in none has religion, at this day, a more distinctly recognized presence, nor more public reverence. When the first bridge was to be opened between Springfield and this town, it was deemed most appropriate that so important an event should be inaugurated by religious exercises, and a sermon from Dr. Lathrop. The annual election sermon in this State; prayer at the opening of the daily session of Congress, and of almost or quite all of the State Legislatures; these, and many similar instances, confirm the justness of the observation. Never can I forget the remarkable scene at the Sumpter meeting held on Union Square, in New York, at the breaking out of our own sad civil war. The immense area, the windows and even the roofs of the surrounding houses were crowded with human beings of all classes; and when, as one of the chaplains, I advanced upon the platform to open the meeting with prayer, every hat was raised, the stillness of a church succeeded, and as I closed, one deep, solemn, almost appalling "Amen" rose from the vast throng and went up to Heaven. Nor can I forget another meeting, hastily gathered on the announcement of President Lincoln's death, at the junction of Wall and William streets, the very mart of trade; the centre and home, it might be called, of the moneyed operations of the entire continent, and even of half the world; the place where Mammon holds his court. Men of all ranks filled the streets, as far as the eye could reach. And when again I was invited to open the meeting with prayer from the portico of the Custom House, profound solemnity reigned, and as I closed by repeating the Lord's Prayer, the whole multitude responded, and their "Amen" seemed to attest the faith as well as the feelings of the country, flying in affliction from all human trust to "Our Father in heaven." I thought that while such a spirit prevails, our institutions are safe; nor need the Church or State require that Christianity shall be established by law, and formally engrafted into our political constitution; nor doubt that our Fathers' God will be the God of their children after them.

No commemoration would seem to be more strictly secular than that of a town charter. But it would be a strange thing to exclude the chapter on religion from the history of any New England town, for thereby the record would often keep out of sight the most interesting and important agency that has been at work in the process. Care has been taken, therefore, that this element shall have its place in the present celebration, and I appear, by your kind invitation, as a former pastor of the old parish, to give the discourse on the occasion. It will not be a formal sermon; and yet, as we follow the current of time, I think we shall meet many things calculated to awaken deep, serious reflections. I cannot disguise from myself the thought, that we are engaged in performing the funeral rites, and raising the monument, and inscribing the epitaph over a century of years.

West Springfield, stretching along the west bank of the river, occupies one of the most beautiful portions of the Connecticut valley. The river, the noblest in New England, from its northern beginning, through its long course to the Sound, presents a great variety of scenery; but at no point, as it seems to me, is it so attractive as here. We can easily imagine the surprise and delight with which the first comers from the East were filled as they reached the summit of Springfield Hill, and the eye took in the river and rich meadow-lands below, and swept the horizon, from the northern limit of vision, down along the hills at the west, and for many miles away to the south, roaming over a picture of surpassing loveliness. The morning and noonday sun brings out its varying features with fine effect, and the beholder might almost fancy himself to be standing upon one of the Delectable mountains. Yet I think several views from the west side of the river, if not so bold and extensive, are even more simply beautiful. Often have I stood, almost entranced, upon the Meeting House Hill, and surveyed the fields and meadows around, clothed with a luxuriant vegetation; Mount Tom at my left, that has reared his hoary front to the suns and storms of a thousand years; the peaceful river, gliding away at my feet, and below, on my right, expanding into a beautiful lake, where lately the rowers competed for the prize; before me Springfield, now showing its many spires, and the Armory its acropolis; and Longmeadow, though far away, still visible on the distant horizon. And how still and Sabbath-like the air! How verdant and quiet this Goshen beneath, hidden away from the bustling world! How rural their dwellings, embowered in foliage, and overarched by those majestic elms! "How goodly are thy tents, O Jacob, and thy tabernacles, O Israel! As the valleys are they spread forth, as gardens by the river's side, as the trees of lingaloes which the Lord hath planted, and as cedar trees beside the waters." Surely the people of this happy valley have a favored heritage, and these are the abodes of thrift and contentment and love. And so it might be, but they are the children of Adam, who, even in Paradise, stretched out his hand to the unpossessed and forbidden thing.

The town of Springfield, including at that time the whole settlement, first had, and until 1640, i. e. five or six years after its occupancy, it retained the Indian name of Agawam. The name Springfield was given, as some say, out of compliment to Mr. William Pynchon, the leader of the band who came from Springfield, near Chelmsford, England. According to others, it was so called, from the springs and streams which abounded in the region. Names were given to their new possessions by the early settlers from various reasons, and often capriciously. Many Old Country names are repeated here; many are derived from something peculiar in their localities, as Brookfield, Longmeadow, Greenfield; and in many cases the Indian appellatives were retained, almost always with advantage for beauty of sound, and descriptive meaning. Thus, in this neighborhood, "Pawcatuck," the western brook and village of the town, means "clear water." "Chicopee," "birch bark place." "Agawam," "crooked river," or "low meadow land." "Mittineaque," "swift water." "Ramapogue," is uncertain and unknown.

The place was reached thirteen or fourteen years after the landing of the Pilgrims, and the settlement of Plymouth Colony, in 1620. In the short interval they had spread abroad and founded the colonies of Salem and Charlestown in 1628, and Boston in 1630. In that year a large number of immigrants, in ten or twelve ships, reached Boston, and complaints began to be made of over population, and the cry was heard, "Give place that we may dwell, for the place is too strait for us." "The inhabitants of Massachusetts," says the historian, "were over-pressed with multitudes of new families that daily resorted thither, so as like a hive of bees overstocked, there was a necessity that some should swarm out." A lively idea is thus afforded of the extent of the Puritan movement in England, as well as in this country. But, certainly, there is something very amusing in the idea of an inconvenient crowding of population at that early date, and with such wide territories all around them. To relieve the great pressure, however, as we must suppose, application was made to the General Court, for leave to advance to the Connecticut and form a new settlement there, which was granted. About 1633, they reached the Great river, (Quonnecticut,) so called by the Indians, not so much from its size or length, probably, as from the number of smaller streams which flow into it along its course, and swell its volume. Windsor, the first settlement in Connecticut in 1633, Hartford in 1635, and New Haven in 1638, were peopled by emigrants from Dorchester; Springfield about 1635, by those from Roxbury. Northampton was purchased from the Indians in 1653, by Mr. John Pynchon, for one hundred fathoms of wampum and ten coats and some trifles besides. Westfield was settled about 1660. From these movements we get an idea of a company of surveyors rather than of permanent inhabitants. They were the pioneers of the wilderness. Thus were they on the march to fulfill the destiny which Divine Providence seems to have appointed for them, and for this country; first to people New England with sons begotten in their own likeness, and then to pour forth, north and west and south, with ceaseless migration, and interfuse themselves among all the other peoples on the continent, becoming, wherever they go, an element of intelligence, enterprise and progress.

As the motive which induced them to seek the Connecticut was the report of the rich lands in its neighborhood, the west bank naturally first attracted them. The Indians esteemed land on this side more valuable than on the other. Their first building was in what, from that circumstance, is known as "Home Meadow Lot" in the present Parish of Agawam. But being warned by the friendly Indians, and probably finding from experience that there they would be exposed to floods, they returned to the east side and made that their homestead. They formed fifteen articles of agreement: *a constitution*, you perceive; the American principle that from the beginning has been introduced into all our municipal, State and general governments; and the spirit which predominated in their mind appears from the fact that the very first article of their compact related to the settlement of a minister. They apportioned the land of which they had become possessed, with rigid impartiality, giving to each settler a home-lot and meadow and wood-lot extending eighty or one hundred rods up the hill, and also a meadow-lot on the west side of the river, as nearly opposite to the home-lot as possible. But the actual, permanent settlement of West Springfield, after the failure at Agawam, was not until 1654 or 5. It was on Chickopee Plains; so that the real original settlement of this town seems to have been above Meeting-House Hill; from there they spread below the hill, and into what is now known as Agawam. The whole town of Springfield, on both sides of the river, was originally twenty-five miles square, including what is now the whole of Holyoke, West Springfield, Agawam, Westfield, Suffield, and nearly all of Southwick on the west, and Springfield, Enfield, Somers, Wilbraham, Ludlow and Longmeadow on the east; a large tract, now teeming with an industrious population. To the honor of the first settlers, it should also be recorded that their possessions were secured not only by legislative grants, but by what was regarded by both parties as a fair purchase from the Indians. What were the equivalents in all cases we do not know; and no doubt at the present time the most valuable would appear ridiculous. Trinkets, strings of wampum for miles of beautiful and fertile lands, seem like simply cheating the natives. But the purchase recognized Indian rights, and the parties appear to have been satisfied. An anecdote is given by Dr. Dwight in his travels, upon what he thought good authority, to this effect: That in the early history of West Springfield, one of the planters, a tailor, had purchased from an Indian chief, for some small equivalent, a tract of about three miles square of some of the best land in the region. Another planter, a carpenter, had constructed a clumsy wheelbarrow, and after careful deliberation and bargaining the tailor took the wheelbarrow in exchange for his land. If this was a fair bargain between whites, it would have been gratuitous knavery to have gone about to cheat the Indians. Troubles and wars, we know, soon arose between the whites and the aborigines all over New England. It was a result simply natural, and perhaps absolutely necessary, or at least unavoidable. The two races could not co-exist on the same soil. Jealousy of the white man soon stimulated the Indian to secret plots and open violence, which incensed the whites in turn to retaliation, and wrong was revenged by wrong. In the French war, the Canadian French subsidized and inflamed them against the English; the Pequot and King Philip's wars; and in this vicinity the burning of Springfield in 1675, so that only four or five houses were left; the massacres at Hadley and Deerfield,—these were parts of the fearful tragedy. The flame which finally spread all over the country was the funeral pyre of the red man's race, and the means, dreadful, often, but certain, of the white man's ascendancy. But whatever wrongs there may have been, the unrequited seizure of their inheritance was not among them.

Although Springfield was the homestead, yet West Springfield seems to have early become, and even until between 1810 and 1820 it continued to be, the leading town—the largest in population in the old County of Hampshire, which included the area now divided into the three river counties, Springfield, Northampton and Hadley ; and, in fact, in 1662 the whole western part of the State. I have not the statistics previous to 1695. At that time West Springfield had two hundred inhabitants in thirty-two families. In 1756, in the March of which year Dr. Lathrop commenced his pastorate of sixty-five years' continuance, the population was between 500 and 600, i. e., it had a little more than doubled in about sixty years. But the following comparison may surprise you. In 1790, West Springfield had a population of 2,367 ; an increase of four-fold in about thirty-four years. Westfield had 2,204; Conway, 2,290 ; Northampton, 1,628, and Springfield 1,574, the smallest of all. West Springfield was the largest, and exceeded Springfield by about 800. This explains the prominence which West Springfield held, not only in this region but throughout the Commonwealth. It was the leading town in Western Massachusetts, and hence its historical influence. The census of 1810 showed it to be still in advance by 400. But fifty or sixty years have wrought a great change. In 1870 the tables are turned. West Springfield had in that year 2,606 inhabitants ; Westfield, 6,679 ; and Springfield, 26,703. This was owing to obvious causes. Springfield was, from the first, the trading centre, which naturally concentrates population ; and West Springfield was a farming district, which implies a sparse settlement. The Armory, established in 1794, also brought operatives together ; and then the railroads since 1839 have made it the centre of an immense business. Yet the preponderance of Springfield was in some respects more apparent than real ; for if we bring into the calculation, as we fairly should, the inhabitants of Holyoke and Agawam, new towns formed out of the old, we shall find a population covering the ancient territory of West Springfield, not so very far behind that of Springfield in numbers.

The first parish of West Springfield was constituted the 27th of May, 1696, and the first church was organized in June, 1698, about sixty years after the settlement of the place. Two things seem to be implied in this statement: First, that with Puritan piety, their religious organization was first attended to, as it preceded the incorporation of the town by nearly eighty years; and secondly, that before that time they were accustomed to cross the river to worship in Springfield, which was regarded as the home. The application to the General Court at Boston, to authorize them to form a separate parish, brings this latter fact very strongly to light. It enlarges upon the inconvenience and danger to which they were subjected by being obliged to cross the river, and the General Court, with commendable caution, and in the quaint phraseology of the day, resolved to nominate "indifferent men," who should adjudicate and settle the matter.

The oldest burying-ground is said to have been given to the parish by a Mr. Foster. The oldest grave-stones found there are dated in 1711 and 1712; but there must have been many interments previous to that time in the ground in Springfield, which must have the oldest burying-place, and the oldest monuments, probably, in all Western Massachusetts.

The first meeting-house was occupied in 1702. It was located on the Common, near where the new Park Street meeting-house now stands, and almost in front of this new Town House. It was forty-two feet square by ninety-two feet high, in humble imitation, one might think, of the tower of Babel, and well calculated to cause a shudder in all lovers of elegant, architectural proportions. It had three roofs, going up to a point, and doors on three sides. There the people met each Sabbath and on public days, for just one hundred years; for about forty years by sound of drum. In 1743, a bell was procured, which was once recast, and on the opening of the new meeting-house was placed in its steeple. The first minister was Rev. Mr. Woodbridge; the second, Mr. Hopkins; both able and popular men in their day, and both bearing names that in succeeding generations have been conspicuous and honored in the theological and educational annals of New England. From the ungainly pulpit of that ungainly house they preached the Word with all fidelity; Mr. Woodbridge for twenty, and Mr. Hopkins for thirty-five years; and from it, also, were delivered by Dr. Lathrop many model sermons, among the most sensible and excellent in matter, singularly clear and simple in arrangement, and classical in style, ever preached in New England, as his published volumes attest. No man of his day, probably, wrote as many and as good sermons as he. He was said to have written 5,000; thus proving that that farming community was not so rude and unlettered that their minister lacked stimulus for study and exertion; it has ever been thus in West Springfield; and showing also that he was not so sluggish as to allow his position to tempt him to indolence in his great work. Indeed, in mind, in industry, in influence, and success, he was one of the foremost men in the land. Not more diligently did the people cultivate their fields than he his spiritual charge, which by such husbandry became "a field which the Lord hath blessed." Besides the volumes given to the press, he left large stores of manuscript sermons, which, for years after, were accustomed, in the absence of their minister, to be read by his son at deacons' meetings, and always to the satisfaction of the old people, who seemed by the reader and the sermon to be carried back to the days when the venerable man himself stood before them. I always felt quite comfortable, when necessarily absent, in the assurance that the people would not lose by a deacons' meeting and a good sermon from Dr. Lathrop's pile; and I am not certain the people did not sometimes have the same feeling.

The singular old structure, in time became so dilapidated

that the winds and the rain had free entrance and exit. It is said, that at a public meeting the rain came down so abundantly that a member proposed they should adjourn under the trees for shelter. And if a pleasant satirical poem, by Dr. Lathrop, was to be literally interpreted, the geese and the cattle found comfortable quarters during the week, where the Christians worshiped on the Sabbath. A copy of this poem was given to me by the late 'Squire Samuel Lathrop, and the good-humored ridicule seemed to have had a happy effect. But diversity of views and wishes as to its location, prevented the building of a new meeting-house for a long time, and somewhat endangered the peace of the Society. The controversy was at length composed by the wise agency of Dr. Lathrop, and by the gift of Mr. John Ashley, which now forms the Parish fund, and was bestowed on the conditions that all parties would agree to the location he should select, and that the meeting-house should remain there for a hundred years. It was opened in 1802, and has endured for seventy-two of the prescribed term of years. Thus came the church on the hill, which became thenceforth the Hill of Zion and the hill of peace. The building contract was for $1,400 and ten gallons of good rum! The pews were occupied by families according to the arrangement of what was called a Seating Committee; the aged persons having the preference, and being advanced towards the pulpit. A mark of respect, and perhaps, also, a gentle reminder that they were getting on in years, and needed to pay particular attention to the words of the preacher. A lot in Agawam meadows is still known as the "Seatin lot," from the fact that the committee, while resting from their work at noon, (beavering, I think they call it,) gathered under the elms and seated the meeting-house. A very primitive and even Old Testament mode of doing business! The seats were free; but every one was taxed for the support of the standing order, unless he signed off; i. e., declared himself to be a member of some other society, to which he paid taxes. (This law was altered or annulled, I think, while I was settled here.) The standing order was the Congregational; exclusive of the Episcopalians, Baptists and Methodists. Moreover a fine was imposed upon such as absented themselves for a certain time from the regular Sabbath services, and hence the remark, that one went to meeting often enough to save his fine. These and like practices, and the fact that the authorizing and bounding of parishes, i. e., in reality the establishment of churches was a prerogative of the General Court, show how strong a hold the ideas and ways of England still kept over the minds of the colonists. Nor need it create surprise. Men do not, at a bound, reach the goal of final right on any subject, and as little do they emancipate themselves in a moment from old ideas and customs. The truth is that the separate spheres of church and state, and real "freedom to worship God" according to the dictates of one's own conscience, were principles to which no party of the Reformers or of that age had fully attained. Not the established church of England, surely. Not the Puritans, as portions of their history show; nor the Presbyterians of Scotland, for there is as much truth as sarcasm in Milton's words, "New Presbyter is but old Priest writ large." Those great thoughts grew into principles and usage much later, after many struggles and only on this soil; nor are they everywhere nor yet in perfect practical operation, even among ourselves.

This connection prompts me to say a few words in regard to the ministry of early New England, and their successors. The ministers were, as a general thing, men of decided ability, or they could not have stood foremost in the great enterprise in hand; men of learning, and many of them of superior culture. They had received all the training the Universities could give; had taken the several degrees which attested their proficiency, and had had regular ordination, and some of them held prominent places in the church of England before they broke from its fold and came to the New World. As far then, as they were leaders, and no other class was so much so, the Puritans were not led, nor was New England settled, by a rabble of vulgar, ignorant fanatics, while the great sentiment which guided their course naturally ennobled them and their deeds. Religion was the motive power, and not commercial gain. A marvelous intensity of religious convictions, which in our day we can scarcely understand, and regard perhaps as only a strange scrupulosity about matters indifferent and trivial; these religious convictions, which could not be quelled, and would brook no compromise, God infused into their souls, to impel them to break the strong ties of kindred and country, to tempt the ocean in miserable ships, and to plant themselves on the edge of a wilderness behind which stretched out a vast continent, on whose very borders, even at their entrance, they seemed to hear the command that they should go up upon the length and the breadth of the land to possess it. One spirit animated pastors and people. No colonists, of whom history gives us any record, were ever impelled by such a spirit, and guided by such leaders. With their piety the ministers brought their learning; their trained habits of thinking, and of careful preparation for their duties. With their learning they brought their books; in some instances, libraries containing volumes of profound research and rare value—the best erudition of the age. Education was a necessity of State. An educated ministry was one of the stones laid at the very foundation of the edifice they reared. To provide for this object, and for the education of their children, was Harvard College founded as soon as possible, and ever since, education has been a cardinal point, a glory of New England, and an educated ministry indispensable.

But they were not a morose class, although the position and work of the first generation might well make them very serious. We smile, indeed, to read of the set, and very formal, solemn manners which existed, for example, in President Edwards' family. Such formality and precision, it is true, were quite common; the virtue of reverence was inculcated upon the young with great care; but these manners did not eradicate human nature; rather they raised and refined it; while the humor, the anecdotes we read of, the pleasantry, the wit which abounded in the social intercourse of many of the old ministers, prove that their real piety was not an enemy to domestic and social enjoyment; that a timely laugh, and even a joke, were not the unpardonable sin. "A large, roundabout common sense" was conspicuous in their ways. There was a large infusion of this element, combined with great vivacity of spirit, that relieved the strength and dignity of his character in Dr. Lathrop. Many stories of his genial humor and keen, ready wit, circulate in the parish to this day. His physical and moral proportions seemed in happy accord.

They employed the press freely, and by that means supplied very useful reading to the people in the scantiness or absolute want of reading matter from other sources; for as yet reading rooms were unknown, bookstores rare, and newspapers very few. True they wrote and published chiefly upon theological themes; they were the absorbing topic, and imbued the community with principles and kept them thinking. And this accounts perhaps, in a measure, for the noticeable cast of the New England mind, even yet; its tendency to discussion; to moral, political, metaphysical, religious and irreligious speculations. The Mathers; Shepherd, of whose writings I have in my library two ancient volumes, one published in London in 1655, the other in 1659; Stoddard; and of the generations following, Edwards, Bellamy, Hopkins, Dwight, Lathrop,—these were a few of the men whose work exerted a powerful influence in their own day, and live and are likely to live in coming times. This particular region was eminently favored with such ministers and writers, as also with religious light and revivals promoted by their ministry. "The great awakening" began and prevailed along this valley.

These men as a general thing were not indeed elegant orators. Very few of them, probably, would have been chosen professors of elocution in our colleges. Some specimens of most godly men, of this class, I have known, were about as far from eloquence, in the popular idea of the word, as could well be conceived. And many manuscripts I have seen of Dr. Lathrop's sermons, and of others, written on the smallest sized paper, in a very fine character, and very close lines, (as if paper was very scarce,) would defy all efforts at free reading, not to speak of anything bordering on elocution. But the people were in sympathy with their spirit and their thoughts, and wished no beautifully embroidered screen interposed between them and the truth; they were willing its light and its heat should come, without softening its rays, directly to their consciences and hearts. Their ministers, again, were always abreast of their age, and often in advance of it in wise progress, and beyond denial they were a political as well as a religious power. But rash experiments in government; abrupt and radical upturning in policy; change for the sake of change; endless reforms with no time for the edifice to settle on its foundation; the shaking up of the commonwealth that the dregs might come to the top, such things they neither preached nor favored. Yet here, as all over the land, the revolution met the cordial support of the clergy; as more recently the clergy of the country were almost unanimously on the side of the government in our sad civil war, because they felt the righteousness of the cause. If then your social and political heritage is to be prized beyond that of other lands, let this town, let New England, let the whole country never forget their obligations to the Christian ministry in the seed-time of their State. And if infidelity should sneer and communism scoff at priestly politicians and claim to devise a system better than our own; to rear a temple of civil freedom without a religion and without a God; to establish a community with no law but the unchecked impulse of raving passion, without personal purity, domestic order, social morality; we may boldly reply that but for such agency as the Christian religion and its ministers exerted in our history, we might have had a French revolution but no United States. Nor can our blessings be secured against these and all enemies in time to come, excepting upon the same condition and at the same price of eternal vigilance. The ambition for place and power; the dreadful relaxation of moral bonds; peculations and frauds; admonish us that even now we need a new enforcement of the like agencies. Our morality wanes under the power of a cold, calculating, selfish worldliness.

As Springfield was in the beginning the centre of the whole settlement, the new parishes formed on this side, before West Springfield was incorporated, were styled parishes of Springfield. Thus Agawam (the only portion of the original domain that retains the Indian name) was made a distinct parish in 1737, including what in 1800 was constituted into the parish of Feeding Hills, and was the sixth parish of Springfield; afterwards the second of West Springfield. Ireland parish, so named from the unusual circumstance that a few Irish families were located there, was first united with settlers on the east side in 1750, and formed into the fifth parish of Springfield, afterwards the third of West Springfield. Of ministers living I shall speak of no others than my predecessor and friend, Dr. Sprague, who through his long pastorates here and in Albany, has maintained a popularity equalled by few and excelled by none; whose literary labors have been extensive and valuable, and who, in retired age, still gathers around him the respect and affections of very many friends—the reward of a consistent and useful life.

I told you at the outset that the religious and civil histories were so intertwined as hardly to be separable. They are the one history of the one people. The charter for a separate town was granted by the General Court in 1773–4, 120 years from the permanent settlement at Chicopee Plains, and 78 after the organization of the first parish. I say the charter was granted but in reality it was imposed. For it seems that the application for a separate township came not from West Springfield, but from Springfield, and was carried against the earnest remonstrances of those who were to constitute the new town. The cause of this singular procedure, why the people of Springfield should thus seek separation from their neighbors, is not known. But the fact to which I have referred, that West Springfield about that time was, or was becoming, the more populous and controlling place, may afford a clue to the mystery. If so, Springfield disliked to be ruled, and must have been ambitious to have its own way; and then it must follow that West Springfield liked to rule, and was not ready to part with authority. Simple human nature in both! The limits of the town thus incorporated were fourteen miles in length by four in width. Now they are about six miles in length and four in breadth. It became a town in troublous times. The controversy between the mother country and the colonies, the main point of which was the claim of the colonists that representation should go along with taxation, was reaching its crisis. In 1774 the clouds had already darkened the sky; the thunder had been heard to mutter in the distance; the storm came, and in 1776 the Declaration of Independence ended forever the authority of Great Britain over these States, and created a new star in the constellation of nations, destined ere a century should have rolled away to rise upward in the firmament and shed its influence for good over all the rest,—over the civilized world. We are beginning to realize the import of that act, and the world begins to realize it also. It was not for ourselves alone. It was one of those grand events, arranged by a superintending Providence, both to indicate and to advance the world's progress. Through its working among the nations, thrones have been cast down, and power has been given to the people against civil and ecclesiastical oppression.

It was a thing to be expected, that some internal commotions should appear before the political sea could rock itself to rest. Shay's insurrection in 1786 broke out in this region, and West Springfield was, in part, the theatre of operations, a large force of the insurgents being collected here under Luke Day, who gave the most complete description of a demagogue I have ever heard: "I will do as I please, and other people must do as I say." The insurrection arose, it is said, because of the oppressive debts contracted by individuals and the State during the Revolution, and chiefly, as we may suppose, from the depreciation of values caused by the unredeemable paper currency, the old Continental money. It was soon and easily suppressed; but the cause may teach a valuable lesson to legislators concerning the demoralizing and dangerous effects of an irredeemable currency and financial derangements. To compare great things with small, the French revolution and Shay's insurrection may be cited as cases in point.

One of the most important events to the town and the State, after the giving of the charter, was the erection of the bridge in 1805 by a corporate company. The sermon by Dr. Lathrop to which I have alluded, a great literary curiosity, has this title-page: "A Discourse delivered at Springfield, October 30, 1805, on occasion of the completion and opening of the great Bridge over Connecticut River, between the towns of Springfield and West Springfield. By Joseph Lathrop, D. D., Pastor of the first Church in West Springfield. Second Edition, H. Brewer, Printer, Mass." The text was from Isaiah xlv. 18,—"God himself, that formed the earth and made it, he created it not in vain: he formed it to be inhabited." How apt! Conceive some ancient prophet announcing that sublime text to the Pilgrims on Plymouth Rock! The Scripture the text, their history to be the sermon! The discourse, which displays great ingenuity, is a sort of passage-way for pertinent thoughts from the most widely separated regions, as the bridge itself collects and conveys commodities from the extreme parts of the land.

The lessons inculcated are exceedingly appropriate. The intercourse between the people on the opposite sides of the river for 150 years had been by boats. We may imagine what a wonderful revolution the bridge must have made in the social and business relations of the whole country,—as great, for that day, as the opening of the railroad bridge more recently,—affording a perfect justification of the religious mode of "*improving*" the great occasion, as the phrase is, which never made the bridge less firm and safe, nor more sightly. It was for many years a toll bridge, but is now free and but one of several.

The building of the town-house on the Common, in 1820, was another prominent public event. And one fact of interest in connection with it is, that portions of the first meeting-house, which had stood for 120 years, and was used for public meetings after the meeting-house on the hill was opened, were placed in this edifice. Beams and rafters that had grown up into stately trees while the Indian was yet monarch and the white man had not trodden the soil; which then for one hundred years responded to hymns and sermons; and then, for fifty years more, have reverberated with parochial and town-meeting eloquence. How interesting would it have been if they could have been identified and placed in this new and commodious town-house you dedicate to-day. What a connecting link between savage and civilized life! What tallies notched with the chief events of the settlement! What tales of solemn import; of quaint manners and earnest words and deeds; of the flight of years and the flow of human generations, would they tell into our ears!

But other interesting antiquities there are. Mr. Aaron Day's house on the Common is 120 years old, and near it is said to be a subterranean passage constructed as an escape from the Indians. Mr. Richard Baggs' house in Shad Lane is of an unknown age, but very ancient. The grand old trees are also a striking feature in the appearance of the town. The elms in

Ramapogue street, dug at Baber's swamp in Tatham, were set out by Lewis and Ebenezer Day and John Ely over one hundred years ago. Darius Ely set out the large button-woods in Joseph Morgan's yard in 1782. And if Dr. Johnson's remark was just, that the man who makes a tree to grow where there is none is a public benefactor, their names deserve honorable mention. But the monarch of all is the "big elm" in Shad Lane ; so called because the men living there were all engaged in the shad fishery, and hence it received the most business-like, but least euphonious or pleasing, of all the names in the town. That district, near the bridge, has now become a dense settlement of operatives in Springfield ; and the aspect of the place is undergoing such changes that soon, I fear, the once rural Paradise will cease to be "the loveliest village of the plain." The Big Elm, as 'Squire Heman Day told me, was brought on his shoulders from the Agawam meadows and planted there on his 21st birthday. Three feet above the ground it is 24½ feet in circumference, and its branches shade about half an acre. Planted there in 1776, it is about the same age as the town. It is just as old as our national government, and a beautiful emblem of that tree of liberty that has struck deep its roots into the earth, whose trunk has stood firm and majestic amidst all the storms it has endured, and whose spreading branches cast a healthful shade over the entire continent. "The hills are covered with the shadow of it, and the boughs thereof are like the goodly cedars. She sends out her boughs unto the seas and her branches unto the rivers."

For nearly three quarters of a century, the town experienced few changes. The people met on the Sabbath in devout worship, and at stated times to transact parochial and town business, and elect delegates to the General Court and to Congress. And thus, and in industrial pursuits, the years flowed on. The grave-yards gathered the generations into their silent domains, and sons took the places of their sires. It was so in part. But from a desire to escape the quietude and plunge into more exciting scenes; from natural ambition to better their circumstances, and still more from that restless spirit which has impelled the race onward and still onward, to cover the whole continent and possess its wealth, the young men very commonly left the old homes, to people the receding West. Yet it was not a "sleepy hollow," where life was sunk in lethargy. They were intelligent as well as industrious, and kept informed of what was going on in the world. There was an unusual number of college-bred men here in my day, and I doubt whether any community of the size, was more regardful of the education of the young, or sent to the colleges more young men than West Springfield; the lists comprising many of different professions, and the record of the town in this respect being most honorable.

Within the last twenty-five or thirty years, however, the state of things has greatly altered. Although the soil was adapted to farming, there were, all over the surrounding region, and within the town itself, vast capabilities for manufacturing purposes, which have been utilized, and have wrought extensive changes, not only in the occupations and habits of the people, but to a large degree also in the appearance of the town and the surrounding country. Springfield, nearly up to 1840, had the character of a pleasant inland country town of quite moderate size, chiefly occupying a district of perhaps a quarter of a mile, or a little more in circuit, from the first meeting-house as the centre. A few stores on the main street were frequented by the inhabitants, and the people from the country. There were two churches so far as my recollection goes, possibly three, some very sightly dwellings on the hills, Ames' Paper Factory, the Armory, probably one quarter of its present extent, and there were less than 10,000 inhabitants. The principal hotel was at the corner of Main and Court streets, whence stages started at set times up and down the river, and east and west, delivering their passengers, wearied and worn, at Albany or Boston, in, it may be, twenty hours. I have left West Springfield at midnight, to take the morning boat at Hartford for New York, arriving there in the evening, with great boasting at the wonderfully rapid transit from Springfield to New York in a day. But how has Springfield enlarged the place of her tent, and stretched abroad the curtains of her habitations. It has now a population, I suppose, of about 30,000, churches numerous and costly, elegant residences and capacious stores of all kinds, a fine public library, several able and influential newspapers, long ranges of streets, alive with busy crowds; is the radiating centre of railroads, north and south, and east and west, over which are annually carried millions of freight, and myriads of travelers, showing in a very striking manner the material prosperity, and the moving, bustling energy of American life.

Cabot was a small village, now the seat of large factories, and the home of a large manufacturing community. And so of the Hadleys.

But on this western side the progress has not been less surprising. Holyoke, formerly the Ireland Parish, at the north end of the town, has, within a year, become a manufacturing city, with 14,000 inhabitants, and its valuation has increased from $2,374,566 in 1863, to $8,578,192 in 1873. Mills and machine shops are various and very extensive. Its water works from Ashley's pond cost $250,000; its free bridge nearly $150,000. It has nine churches, eleven school-houses, and land has risen in some localities over 200 per cent. in five years. About 7,000,000 of pressed brick are made there annually.

At the north end of modern West Springfield, Mr. Clark has a flourishing carriage factory, which reminds me to say, that the first wagon known in the town, was without springs, and owned in Amostown. Whoever has suffered by such a conveyance over a rough road, and then has tried Mr. Clark's carriage, and then a drawing-room car over a smooth rail, must be well drilled in the degrees of comparison: positive, misery; comparative, comfort; superlative, enjoyment. Yet the primitive method of going to meeting on horseback, the women on a pillion, could hardly have equaled the springless wagon in comfort.

The water power of the Agawam has also been turned to good account. Mittineaque, begun in 1844, contains 900 inhabitants, being one-third of the whole town, a Congregational and a Catholic church, and four large schools, a cotton mill, employing about 300 hands, three paper mills, manufacturing in the aggregate five tons daily; all grown up on the spot, which, in my time was as wild and unreclaimed as when the savage hunted its forests, or shot his canoe across its waters. Mr. Sewall White, who overflowed with curious and antique lore, was accustomed to relate a tale, not all invented, probably, but received by the early settlers from current tradition; a legend of Indian love which had its seat at Mittineaque. Names and minute circumstances have perished in the lapse of years. But diverse forms of life are really not so opposite, that we cannot in one condition often picture to ourselves the realities of another. We may conceive the Indian beauty, the pride of her village, and the Indian brave, her favored suitor, and follow out a story which needs no vivid imagination to fill up its details of love and plighted faith; of joys and fears; of desertion and jealousy; of frantic passion and wild despair; the "swift waters" at Mittineaque closing at last over the broken-hearted pagan maiden. We do not often recall to our thoughts the truth, that this whole continent had been the theatre, upon which, ere yet the white man came, great nations flourished, and the drama of life was enacted in its twofold forms, both tragedy and comedy; that here were homes in which the affections and sympathies of human hearts, warm and tender as our own, conjugal and paternal and filial love and duty played their part; and that here also, human passions dwelt in savage breasts, and were excited to deeds of grandeur or horror; to heroism and self-sacrifice; to treachery and blood. The ground on which we tread covers a whole people, once numerous and mighty, of whom scarce a vestige remains. Sometimes the names imprinted on the soil remind us that they were here; and tradition, fast fading into mist, tells what they were, and obscurely what they thought, and what they did. The air seems full of voices of the past; of romance unstoried; histories untold; and poetry unsung. Streamlets and groves were often the seats of a mythology as beautiful and imaginative as that of Greece, and the deep forests, of a superstition as stern and cruel as that of the Druids. And many a spot over which we heedlessly wander, has been the scene of sweet home-bred joys, or Spartan fortitude, or more than Roman courage. And many also, could the earth give up her secret of fearful crimes, of desolated homes and crushed happiness. But it was all human still. And there was a religion too. The Great Spirit implied the idea of a God; the Northern Dancers, immortality; the great hunting ground, a conscious, active being beyond the grave; all, no doubt, the shattered fragments of some very ancient tradition brought away, probably, from the early seats of the human family. Could the red man have held the pen, what narratives could he have given of life enacted on this very soil, to show how human nature is evermore the same in its elements, and how truth is stranger than fiction. But the Indian is dispossessed, and from the homes of his tribes, and the graves of his fathers, he pursues his weary journey to the setting sun. Soon he will have disappeared forever from the continent that once was his; and no historian or poet of his own will ever write his story, or chant the funeral dirge of his race. We give our version, not always perhaps the truth, and the term savage is made to mean, whatever is faithless or ferocious among men. But have you ever read a tale of savage barbarity that could not instantly be matched by one of civilized and self-styled Christian men, against their Christian brothers? often, too, under the mask of religion. And oh! how long and fearful the catalogue of wrongs of civilized men against the poor Indian.

But while we thus expend our sympathies, we may be reminded that the Indian was but a modern compared with nations, the monuments of whose civilization and power excite our wonder and baffle our curiosity. All over the continent, but especially through its central regions, their works remain more skillful and imperishable than any the red men have left, and bearing evidence of a higher degree of cultivation. But when and whence they came, and who and what they were, and how they perished, what oracle will proclaim? How strange that in this newly discovered and virgin world we are walking amidst the tombs of many ages, and successive races of men, who here grew great and built cities and have left evidences of military art to prove their title to man's warlike passion, and their Babel towers are ruins, and the builders have made themselves no name to be remembered. Truly "Man is like to vanity." Over this vast tomb is written, "Generation goeth and generation cometh."

The glance we have taken at the changes which have occurred in this town, during the few past years, is full of interest. In place of the one church, we find eighteen or twenty, meaning, as we hope, that religion has kept pace with the advancement in other respects. The population has increased, in the last half of the century, six or seven fold. Three free bridges and two railroad bridges span the river in place of one then within the limits of the town; and all around this rural centre, the throngs of operatives, and the roar of machinery, and the bales of merchandise, and these but a small portion of what the whole State produces, seem to say that New England will soon rival Old England in various fabrics, as Pennsylvania threatens to do with iron. But education in this favored region has advanced in like proportion. Round Hill at Northampton, the Female Academy at South Hadley, the Academies at East

7

Hampton, Westfield, Wilbraham, and Amherst College, all in this vicinity, and all created within the present century, in addition to a full supply of district schools, show the value the people set on education, and that of the higher order. This, and their Puritan principles, have given them their pre-eminence. We can with difficulty estimate the advancement in books, apparatus, school accommodations and modes of instruction at the present day, over the very limited means of education fifty, or even twenty-five years ago. And the discoveries and improvements, particularly in Natural Science, are literally immeasurable. Boys and girls at primary schools are now inducted into learning that was unknown when their grandsires were at college.

And if we raise our eyes from this immediate vicinity, to survey the whole country, what wonders fill our minds. From a narrow strip on the Atlantic coast, the population has spread in fifty years to the base of the Rocky Mountains, filling all the intermediate space with States, many of them larger than several kingdoms of the Old World. They have over-leaped the mountains and poured down the declivities on the west, planting Cities and States on the Pacific shore, and carrying there the principles, the institutions, and the religious conscience, also, which characterized the early colonists in America.

And if, with wider view, we take in the civilized world, we find that the whole has been in motion. In inventions and discoveries affecting almost all departments of industry; in consequent improvement in the conditions of social life; in political changes that promote the true ends of government, and the well-being of the masses of the people; in the introduction of high moral and religious principles into public acts; in thus urging on the race in the path of true progress, the last hundred years have been, probably, the most efficient of all the ages of recorded time. With Galileo we may exclaim," But it does move!" And let us not overlook the fact that in this progress, the idea of right and of duty, in place of mere will and brute force, has been gaining ground. It was consicence; the feeling of obligation to their own conscience and to God: it was Luther's "Here I stand: God help me: I can do no otherwise," that filled and exalted the souls of the Puritans in Engand, the Huguenots in France, the Covenanters in Scotland, to brave all consequences in the maintenance of what they felt to be right. That conscientiousness planted these wastes with religious men, and they have carried it over the continent and have spoken its lesson to other lands. The assertion of principle wrought out our independence. It was to establish justice. And let me add, duty to God and to humanity roused the spirit and stiffened the sinewy arm of the nation in our late civil conflict, to uphold our free constitution, and wipe out forever and forever the stain and the curse of African slavery. I think this idea of conscientious duty runs through our whole history. Plymouth Rock; the monumental granite on Bunker's Hill; the soldiers' monuments in every town, and that beautiful memorial tablet you have so fittingly placed at the entrance of this hall, to commemorate your sons given up at the call of duty, all proclaim that the Puritan principle and spirit have not yet died out.

But strange contradictions appear in human societies. Israel, God's chosen people, was selected from among the nations as the repository of the doctrine of the Divine Unity. Yet their prevailing sin, until the Babylonish captivity, was idolatry. The United States were committed to the doctrine of universal freedom and equal rights for all men. It was the boasted land of liberty. But nowhere, certainly in modern times, was slavery so widely spread and so deadly. I believe God appointed this as the theatre, and brought the two principles face to face, that here the battle might be fought out and the victory proclaimed for all future times and places. And I ever thought the evil was so inveterate that it must end in convulsions and blood. The issue came, and has been settled in our day. When the thunders and lightnings of war ceased, a voice came out from the throne saying, " IT IS DONE." Slavery is ended. This opprobrium is removed henceforth from this fair continent, and it will disappear, in due time and speedily, from all civilized States, in marked reversal of the practices of all former ages and modes of social and political life.

And to America also the honor falls of having under very irritating circumstances, reduced to practical use the Christian idea of international arbitration; reason and right in the settlement of national disputes, in the place of senseless and passionate war. It is a fitting prayer for our nation; evermore let principle and conscience assert their supremacy in all our affairs; let this idea be ingrafted into the fixed sentiments of the people, that reason is better than violence, justice is always politic, that truth is great and will prevail. And this prayer should be reduced to a settled purpose, universal in its application; including all classes of men and all kinds of evil. The broad and massive foundation of our whole national superstructure should be righteousness; then will become manifest to mankind the reason of the being of this republic in the course of human events. The training of the Fathers, under the hard rule of despotism, civil and ecclesiastical; their guidance to this land; their settlement; the revolution; our civil war, and by that means the extinction of slavery; will be seen to have been so many steps by which our nation became prepared to take its peculiar place and speak with high authority of liberty and of justice in the counsels of mankind. Thus events will "Vindicate eternal providence, and justify the ways of God to man."

Here, then, we close our review of the settlement of West Springfield and of the past hundred years of the town. It has been a time of great commotion; and the changes wrought have not been superficial merely, but have reached the foundation of the religious, social and political fabric. Our entire civil polity has been changed; and with the perfect freedom of action now enjoyed, with the path of advancement in various directions opened to the generous ambition of all classes, and with increasing wealth and ease, the sentiments and habits of the people are likely also to undergo great modifications. The character of the generations that are to come after us, will feel these influences even more than we have done. It is to be developed under other conditions than those which existed in the retired life and simple occupations of the Fathers; and the result must be contemplated with solicitude by every Christian patriot and every lover of his race. Will they escape the danger of a low, material civilization? The Fathers served their generations by the will of God, and are fallen asleep. But their life-work remains. Their just thoughts, their religious spirit, their energy and enterprise infused themselves into the young blood of the nation, and their memorial appears in the noble institutions under which we live. Thus far, these institutions have been preserved against trials not a few nor small. They stand, at this day, in a more hopeful condition, in some respects, than at any preceding period; more free from inward contrarieties and outward dangers; better poised on their foundations, and more authoritative before the world. Shall it continue thus? We read the past. The record of a century of struggles and successes, is open before us, and we thank God and take courage. But the future is always uncertain. What eye can pierce the obscurity? what prophetic mind can forecast the events of a century to come? That they will be as momentous in their influence upon the progress of mankind as any that have ever occurred, I fully believe. We have not yet reached the promised land. But we are acting in one of the grand revolutions of time. We are hasting in providence, as I think, to a new order of things, of which only divine prophecy gives us a glimpse. Nor can we fail to ask with anxiety what shall be the place and position of our beloved country in that coming age? And we may answer with confidence, that if the principles which animated the first settlers, if the spirit that was in them be maintained ; if the God they obeyed be revered ; if our children love truth and justice, and practice moderation, amidst the affluence of their advantages, all will be well. Our Republic will then march in the van of the nations, going on to a higher, purer, and altogether a better civilization than any the world has yet known. The bright vision that dawns on our fancy will have become reality ; our hopes will have passed into fruition ; our children will be living amidst the splendor of the golden age of promise, enjoying the blessings the Bible foretells. The days of ignorance, and injustice, and vice, and misrule, and convulsions, and wars will have gone, to be succeeded by prosperity and gladness

"Such as earth saw never,"
"Such as heaven stoops down to see."

"Shall old acquaintance be forgot?" was then sung with excellent effect; prayer was offered by Rev. Dr. Ashbel Vermilye of Schenectady, N. Y.; the long meter doxology rang out grandly in the solemn strains of "Old Hundred," and the benediction, by the orator of the day, concluded the exercises in the hall.

THE FIRST TOWN HALL.

BUILT IN 1820.

THE CENTENNIAL DINNER.

FOLLOWING the hall exercises came the glad news of dinner in the school-room below. The space being limited, only 190 found places at the table, but enough crowded in afterward to make locomotion almost impossible. Col. Aaron Bagg appropriately presided here, as he did in the hall above. Rev. E. B. Clark, of Chicopee, invoked the Divine blessing on the prepared food. The feast ended, the Band played, and the President of the day announced the first regular toast:

"*The Governor of the Commonwealth.*" The response came from the Secretary in the following letter:

BOSTON, March 21, 1874.

MY DEAR SIR:—Your favor with an invitation for me to be present at the anniversary exercises of your town on the 25th ultimo is at hand. Be assured it would give me pleasure to be with you on so interesting an occasion; but my official engagements are such, that it will be impossible for me to accept your kind request. You may well be proud of your history in the past, and I trust the future will be no less eminent. While I am not personally acquainted with many of your townsmen, yet I know how ready you have been to further every good and noble enterprise. May your children be worthy successors of so noble an ancestry.

I am your obedient servant,

W. B. WASHBURN.

"*The Commonwealth of Massachusetts,*" was responded to by Mr. SAMUEL L. PARSONS, of New York:

About two hundred and fifty years ago there landed from the old ship, Mayflower, on the rocky shores of Massachusetts, a company of one hundred and two persons, seeking the freedom that the New World offered, to worship God, and to plant a new nation that might be an honor to the world. The severe winter, exposures, and disease, carried to the grave in four months one-half of the Pilgrim party. But this terrible affliction only served to draw the hearts of those who survived more closely together, and to knit them more firmly in bonds of brotherhood, for the purpose of accomplishing the work the Master had for them to do. The compact formed on the Mayflower was carried into the new State; it is the corner-stone of the institutions that have been handed down to us, and in which we so proudly rejoice to-day. Massachusetts is the leading State in manufactures; she is not behind in the arts; her commerce is of world-wide repute; her statesmen are among the leading minds of the world; her churches and schools are open to the people; her purse is open to the cry of distress from whatever land. Wherever I have traveled, I have found the people not only respect a man from Massachusetts, but they are ready to trust him, believing that true men hail from the old Bay State; indeed her sons are among the leading men in nearly all the States of the Union, and have carried her institutions and energy with them. It is hardly necessary for me to occupy your time further; your own immortal Webster was content to say of Massachusetts, "There she is, behold her." And surely it would be presumption in me, with the added glories of a quarter of a century, not to leave her in that same exalted position.

"*The Orator of the Day,*" called up Dr. Thos. E. Vermilye, of New York City:

Mr. President:—I thank you most sincerely for the complimentary manner in which you are pleased to speak of my services to-day; and I thank this company and the good people of the old town of West Springfield, for the kindness they have shown me to-day, and me and mine in times past. I feel much at home in this region and recall years of pleasant, and I hope not unprofitable residence among you—as the pastor of the old first parish. I have always felt, and often said that my ministerial life and usefulness (if I have been useful in my calling), was greatly formed and made by my pastorate in West Springfield, and my advice to my young brethren would be to prefer such a parish for their first settlement, if they could find it, to any city charge, as the school for their professional training. But, Mr. President, I ought not to indulge such a strain ; and particularly I ought not to occupy the time of this respected company after taxing them already for more than an hour at the public meeting. Let me, however, pay a debt of justice before I sit down. Of course I knew a good deal of West Springfield ; its history, its localities, its men, and many, also, of its peculiarly good things in the way of story and anecdote. But I needed aid in the short time given me for preparation, and for that aid, in the collection of materials, I wish it to be understood that I was indebted very largely to Deacon Bagg, who has taken such a lively interest in this Centennial Celebration ; and who is such an adept in West Springfield lore that what he does not now know of West Springfield, can hardly be greatly worth knowing.

Mr. President, we shall not meet again ; none of us will be here when the next century shall have rolled round. But may they who then shall occupy these places have no reason to chide themselves for any defection from the principles and example of the Pilgrim fathers.

"*Our Brave Soldiers*," was responded to by Rev. E. N. POMEROY, Pastor of the First Church :

MR. PRESIDENT :—Of the soldiers of this town who took part in the three great wars of our nation's history, I cannot now speak particularly. I cannot tell you of their individual exploits, or of their individual sufferings. I cannot even point out the great engagements in which they severally took part ; indeed I can call very few of them by name. I can only speak of them as constituent parts of a mighty force of freemen, who, from farm, and mill, and shop, and bench, and study, and pulpit, and every other place where men support their families, and earn the rights of citizenship, assembled under arms with determination to resist oppression, to suppress rebellion, and to maintain their rights ; and who, after accomplishing their object, returned to their homes and quietly resumed their occupations.

Perhaps the world never witnessed a grander spectacle than that of these earnest, intelligent, and many of them educated men, assembling at their country's call to fight her battles, and to die if need were in her defence; except when it saw the victorious survivors, after these battles were fought, and when the cause was maintained, returning to their families and to the duties of civil life.

But sir, I am not here to pronounce an oration on the virtue and the valor of our soldiers; the occasion does not call for it. The living do not desire our encomiums; the dead do not need our eulogies. It is enough for the former that the integrity of this Union is preserved; that the foundation of this government is established; that the fetters of the slave are broken. It suffices for the latter that their deeds have passed into history; that their names are written in substantial granite, and memorial marble; that their memories are cherished by those who love them, and that, with every returning spring-time, their graves are decorated, and their epitaphs re-written with flowers.

It is, however, especially fitting that our soldiers should be remembered to-day; and in every future centennial celebration; even when this imposing structure shall have given place to one still loftier and grander, may our soldiers receive ever prouder and more honored mention. Without their aid this people could never have become a nation; they had never resisted the aggressions of British tyranny; they might often have declared, but could never have established their independence. It is owing to their valor, in great part, that this nation remains a first-class power; that the sun in the heavens does not look down on "states dissevered, discordant, belligerent;" that the roll-call of slavery has never yet been heard under the shadow of our Bunker Hill Monument, and that it is now quite certain it never will be heard there.

It is commonly considered a great and glorious thing to have fought for one's country; to have stood upon "the perilous edge of battle;" to have flung one's self into "the imminent, deadly breach;" and so it is. But sir, it is a noble and a glorious thing to have done one's duty anywhere. The grandest victories are not those won in deadly strife; the most valiant fighting is not that done on the sanguinary field; the proudest, the supreme moment is not

> "When speaks the signal trumpet tone,
> And the long line comes gleaming on;"

it follows not "the rush of adverse battalions, the sinking and rising of pennons, the flight, the pursuit, and the victory;" it comes rather to a man when through a long course of years, having patiently, persistently, fearlessly done right, at last though only at the close of his mortal career, he sees his life's object accomplished. Not every hero has borne arms in battle; not every soldier has been under fire; not every valiant man has marched to the cannon's mouth; not every conqueror has been crowned with laurel.

> "Peace hath her victories,
> No less renowned than war."

They who incur odium in the discharge of duty; they who refuse to sacrifice principle for pelf or position; they who dare part with reputation if need be to preserve character; they, the vanguard in the army of the Lord, who take and hold positions in advance of the age in which they live; they who are determined and prepared to do their duty though the heavens fall; these, sir, I maintain are the bravest of the brave.

Our soldiers in the Revolution, and in the war of 1812, did their work well; but after peace was finally established, and another conflict with the mother country placed almost beyond a peradventure, it was a harder thing to forgive the past, and to recognize the virtues of the English people. The soldiers who put down the Great Rebellion, covered themselves with glory; but it will be a grander victory than that achieved at Vicksburg, at Gettysburg, or at Richmond, when, remembering that our foes were our brothers, and that their valor was not inferior to our own, we can erase from our standards the records of the conflict and forgive and forget the past.

All honor, then, not to our soldiers only, but to all our heroes.

> "Yea, let all good things await
> Him who cares not to be great,
> But as he saves or serves the State.
> Not once or twice in our great nation's story,
> The path of duty was the way to glory.
> He that walks it, only thirsting
> For the right; and learns to deaden
> Love of self, before his journey closes,
> He shall find the stubborn thistle bursting

Into glossy purples that outredden
All voluptuous garden roses.
Not once or twice in our fair country's story,
The path of duty was the way to glory.
He, that ever following her commands,
On with toil of heart and knees and hands,
Through the long gorge to the far light has won
His path upward and prevailed,
Shall find the toppling crags of duty scaled
Are close upon the shining table-lands
To which our God Himself is moon and sun.
Such were they; their work is done:
But while the races of mankind endure,
Let their great example stand
Colossal, seen of every land,
And keep the soldier firm, the statesman pure,
Till in all lands and through all human story
The path of duty be the way to glory.
And let the land whose hearths they saved from shame,
For many and many an age proclaim
At civic revel and pomp and game,
And when the long illumined cities flame,
Their ever-loyal, noble soldier's fame,
With honor, honor, honor to them,
Eternal honor to their name."

"*The Old School-House*," was responded to by Rev. ASHBEL G. VERMILYE, D. D., of Schenectady, N. Y., son of the orator of the day:

My own recollections, Mr. Chairman, run back about forty years, when I was here as the "minister's son." In that old "school-house" next door, which you have made the subject of this toast, I, with other boys, received some old-fashioned floggings. Peace to the ashes of Mr. Dutch—they were well laid on. To-day, after forty years, I bear him witness, as one who knew how to touch up the boys, and inculcate sound learning. But to-day, sir, the old school-house looks gloomy; as if it were saying to itself—nevermore! I suppose it must now come down—perhaps it would rather, since there will be none in it any more to give or take a taste of the birch.

Even in so quiet a town, I find few, as forty years have left their marks and changes. The elms and the river are, indeed, about the same; Nature only notches her centuries. And I suppose the katydid still makes music in the trees for boys put to bed in the dark, as the little creatures did for me. But I see you have since fenced in the old "Common" out here, where on Sunday evenings after sundown the youngsters used to kick foot-ball: usually selecting the part in front of the minister's house, how much to his edification I do not know; I can only speak for his son, whose eyes saw from a distance what he was not permitted to join in, and whose ears also (let me say) sometimes caught the sound of the wash-tub, just under the hill. Also, they did their courting on Sunday evening; though, for that matter, probably it is the same now. That is a business not subject to the mutations of time and tide. Empires may rise and fall, rivers may lapse and run dry, but never the course of courting.

In those antique days, as they will seem to some, we made our way to Springfield by a little steam-boat with the wheel behind. I remember that the old "Oliver Ellsworth" had to back off seven times, where the river joins the Sound; and then, unable to get through, had to put back to New Haven short of wood! From this you may realize the stride of time and change. Why, sir, two years ago I met the man, a Mr. Harrod, who probably introduced the tomato (then called "love apple") as an edible into the country. And here I may tell you what I think is an unpublished anecdote of Dr. Lathrop (or Lotrop, as the people called him), but which I heard when a boy. Dr. Lathrop had obtained and planted, (the first hereabout) some seeds of that new luxury, the water-melon. But to his sheer annoyance, just as they were ripe, some wicked depredator carried them all off, and moreover cut his vines to pieces. However, if he was in "meeting" the next Sabbath, as he most likely would be, and had any conscience left—which, it must be confessed, stealing from a minister would hardly indicate—he doubtless got the worst of it; for the Doctor gave an excoriating sermon from the apt text: "When thou comest into thy neighbor's vineyard, then thou mayest eat thy fill at thine own pleasure; but thou shalt not put any in thy vessel."

You, Mr. Chairman, will easily recall some things that are fixed in my boyish remembrances—the old foot-stoves, the open Franklin stoves, and brass fenders, the warming-pans and such like; but one old custom sticks to my memory, because it caused an awkward catastrophe to a relative of mine. It was the habit they had in "meeting" of chewing dill, not because the minister was sleepy, but because they were; and then of throwing the stems into the carpetless aisle. Through that dill my relative, to his great mortification as a city young man, came to a fall; nor did he relish any better the next accident (for it was such) and the general titter which followed, when my father gave out a hymn, two verses of which had in them something about making his standing more secure than it was before he fell!

In closing, sir, I would just recall, but with undiminished respect, a name or two of that day—among the Elys that of Justin, so unfailingly kind, so good; and then, 'Squire Samuel Lathrop who in face and form and mien always reminded me of Washington, and if I could go back farther, I should well like to speak of Rev. Jonathan Parsons (Whitefield's friend) who was born here. But this was an admirable parish in both men and women. There were here women who shed a luster upon their bygone names—Charity, Mercy, Patience, Prudence and the like; I think the town never produced but one Silence, and she was under ground before my day. She was a Champion while living, and I guess was buried with the "belt." My friend Parsons spoke of the past this morning, in contrast with the present, as the "mummy" state of the town. I think he was mistaken. When the tomb of James Otis, the patriot orator, was opened, they found the roots of the great Paddock elm enfolding his skull. So are the roots of your present prosperity to be found, inseparably entwined with the skulls, resting in the homes and the homely virtues, of those who went before you, and now lie entombed under the shadows of your spreading elms. If other causes you would seek, turn with gratitude, as for one I do, to the old church and the old school-house.

"*Springfield, the Mother of Towns.*" Hon. J. M. STEBBINS, Mayor of Springfield, responded:

I am happy to announce to you that the mother of West Springfield is usually well, in fact, she is always pretty well. After two and a quarter centuries of active life, she is just entering upon the early stages of a noble womanhood. She has some promising daughters of whom she is proud, and some grand-daughters, Agawam and Holyoke, one of whom aspires to be larger than her mother. Still she is apparently young and more vigorous than ever. She grows in graces as she grows in years. We, who ought to be her friends, think we see in her daily new virtues and attractions by which she draws us more closely to her.

West Springfield is one of her oldest daughters, and was the most perverse and refractory of all the members of the family. She persisted in chosing her man to represent the old town in the General Court, when the whole family voted together, and more than once succeeded in doing it. The mother town wished to be represented by John Bliss and John Worthington, and West Springfield wanted her man. The indignant mother called to her aid her sons from the Springfield mountains, who voted down the candidate of her disobedient daughter. At the next session of the General Court, at the mother's request, West Springfield, against her protest, was turned out of doors, and became a town against her own will—a thing unparalleled in town history. A punishment of a hundred years has satisfied the forgiving mother, who has almost forgotten her daughter's offences, and now, after a century, it is whispered, the daughter is penitent, and is looking wistfully back into the old household, and there are hints of a ninth ward. Let her put herself in order, protect her dike from muskrats and the south winds in flood-time, build her school-houses, water-works, side-walks, pave her streets, and behave, and there can be no doubt the kind mother will take her back.

West Springfield has been fortunate in many things. Her old men remembered her fruit-bearing orchards, her fat cattle, heavy fields of grass and rye, and her young men have seen and felt the influence of her gold-bearing fields of corn and tobacco. But especially has she been fortunate in her preaching and the character of her preachers. In Springfield we were not quite so fortunate in our first preacher, but we have had a vast deal of law. One of the earliest trials by jury was that in which the Rev. Geo. Moxon, our first preacher recovered a verdict of £6 against John Woodcock, for slander. None of your preachers ever needed to have their good names polished up before a jury. But this was in 1640. Since then our ministers have been shining lights in the churches and faithful guides to the people.

I was requested to speak of the bridge across the Connecticut River, which was built in 1805, partly to reconcile the mother and daughter. For a century and a half the inhabitants of the old town were separated by the river, which in freshets swept over the meadows and some of the settled parts of West Springfield now protected by dikes. Crossing by the three ferries was often dangerous—sometimes impossible. In the latter part of the last century, some visionary young men were bold enough to agitate the question of a bridge. It was talked of and delayed for years. The old men had seen freshets and great masses of ice in the river. One said if a bridge was built it would not stand, others said it could never be done—they might as well think of bridging the Atlantic Ocean. The old men died and then the young men built the bridge.

The *Federal Spy*, published October 29, 1805, has the following:

"The elegant bridge erected over Connecticut River in this town, will be opened on Wednesday (to-morrow), *one toll free.* We understand there will be a sermon preached by Dr. Lathrop, a procession formed, cannon fired, a ball in the evening, and that, in fact, it will be a day of glee."

The sermon was preached, and the procession was formed, and when it reached the bridge, a salute of seventeen guns was fired, which was three times repeated from both ends of the bridge. Three thousand people were present. It was a day of jubilee. The newspaper the week after says:

"The bridge is so constructed with frames upon piers, connected by long timbers with the arches that the traveler passes over nearly the whole extent of it, on an elevated plane, affording a view of extensive landscapes, in which are blended well cultivated fields, plains and villages, river and meadows, lofty mountains, and indeed a variety in the beauties of nature which is highly gratifying to the eye."

We hardly see in the bridge that now spans the river, an "elevated plane" or "elegant structure." The old men were half right. The young men could not or did not build a bridge that would stand. The old red bridge "gave way and fell to the water," July 19, 1814. The fall is said to have been caused by the passage of heavy army wagons, many of which had crossed the year before. It was rebuilt and completed

October 1, 1816. It was carried away in a flood in March 1818. Two piers at the west end were left standing,—five were swept away. It was just after the war. The times were hard, no money could be had to rebuild the bridge. The people might have been discouraged if the evil one had not come to their aid. What he was doing to help them appears from this advertisement:

"Springfield Bridge Lottery.—Who will complain of Hard Times when $1,500 may be had for $3. The Drawing is near at hand."

The two last bridges were built partly from the profits of lotteries.

The fight to make it free was fought almost as long and valiantly as that to make the slave free. Worthy friends of freedom often defeated, as often renewed the battle, till at last they conquered—but not till long after the slave had become free, did the bridge become "toll free" as it was advertised to be on the day of its opening. A petition to the City Council asks that a covered way be extended along both sides of the bridge on the outside. And so the bridge—the only thing but the river between us—is still the subject of discussion as it has been for the last century—and likely to be for the next. In the next, we may hope there will be better men and women, better laws and manners, new and higher wants, and greater means of gratifying them. Men are not running down,—the fountains of life are not drying up. Customs, manners, amusements, habits change; but men are no worse.

In the next century, I have no doubt, there will be better men than there were in the last—than there are now. They will be more intelligent, and have better food, clothing, houses, and have more comforts than we. They will want nearly the same things, as human nature and wants may not change. They will use more and better water, and have better wine at the Sacrament, and we and our children will preserve, I hope, the old love that has existed so long between us, and the old bridge, too, which has been a faithful servant to us both, till we build a better one.

"*The Founders of Springfield,*" was responded to by Hon. HENRY MORRIS, of Springfield, Mass.:

MR. PRESIDENT:—It is perhaps proper, as my friend the Mayor has spoken for the mothers of towns, that I should say a few words for the fathers of towns. And in responding for those who were the fathers and founders of Springfield, I feel that I speak of men who were truly noble.

Foremost among them, of course, was William Pynchon. He came over from England with Governor Winthrop, and before he settled here on the Connecticut River, he founded the town of Roxbury, once a historic name, but recently merged and lost in the poorer one of Boston Highlands.

Mr. Pynchon held for several years the office of Assistant in the Colonial government, and was for a time its Treasurer, both offices of high honor and responsibility.

He removed from Roxbury to the Connecticut River, that he might carry on to advantage the fur trade with the Indians, in which he was largely engaged. Here he established the "Plantation of Agaam," as Springfield was at first called. So long as he remained here he was the only magistrate, and, with the assistance of a jury of six men, tried the causes and decided the controversies of the Plantation.

In all the public affairs of the settlement, municipal and ecclesiastical, he exercised a controlling influence, wisely and usefully.

With Mr. Pynchon came his son-in-law, Henry Smith, a man of education and ability, who, when Pynchon left, was appointed a magistrate in his place, but soon after abandoned Springfield and went to England.

Elizur Holyoke was another prominent settler, and took a leading part in all the affairs of the town. He married a daughter of Mr. Pynchon. It was upon her monument that the lines were inscribed—

> "She that lies here was, while she stood,
> The very glory of womanhood."

He was the father of Capt. Samuel Holyoke, a young man, who in the celebrated Falls fight, when our men were attacked by an overwhelming force of Indians, and Capt. Turner, the commander, was killed, took command of our men and successfully conducted the retreat. He is said to have killed six of the Indians with his own hand.

Then there was Deacon Samuel Chapin, the ancestor of all the Chapins, including my friend of the Massasoit House, present here to-day. He held many offices of trust and responsibility in the town.

Samuel Wright, also a deacon, was a leading man in the church. He removed to Northampton, and died there.

Jehu Burr, who came with Mr. Pynchon from Roxbury, was a carpenter, and probably made the identical wheelbarrow for which the tailor sold him three miles square of land in West Springfield, as we were told by the Reverend orator to-day.

Another influential man was Rev. George Moxon, the first minister of the place. He was an old friend of Mr. Pynchon, with whom he returned to England in 1652. My friend, the Mayor, has held him up to censure, because he sued John Woodcock, one of his parishioners, for slander. I do not think the minister quite deserved the censure. It was his misfortune to be called as a witness in a trial in Connecticut, in which Woodcock, who was a mischievous fellow, was a party, and Woodcock charged him among his people with having been guilty of perjury on that occasion. Mr. Moxon sought to vindicate his character from this aspersion, and he did so by the verdict of a jury, which rebuked the slanderer.

Near the latter part of Mr. Moxon's ministry, suspicions of witchcraft began to be entertained in Springfield. A poor woman, living at the lower end of our Main street, who had killed her own child, and was probably insane, was accused of bewitching Martha and Rebecca Moxon, the minister's daughters, and was taken to Boston for trial upon the double charge of witchcraft and murder. She was acquitted of the witchcraft, but convicted of the child murder. This trouble, and his friendship for Mr. Pynchon, probably induced Mr. Moxon to accompany him to England, and he never returned to America.

I must not omit to name as one of the most influential of the founders of Springfield, John Pynchon, the son of William. When the father went back to England the son remained here, and soon succeeded to all, and more than all, his father's influence and honors. He was a man of very superior character, and, during nearly the whole of his long life, performed the duties of a magistrate, military commander, and civil leader in the town. To no man of those early days does this part of the State owe more than to John Pynchon.

"*Our Contributions to Missions,*" was responded to by EDWIN BLISS, D. D., of Constantinople, Turkey:

In claiming me here to-day, Mr. Chairman, as one of your "Contributions to Missions," you help me to answer a question which has sometimes puzzled me; namely, where I belong. Born in Vermont, bred in old Springfield, the other side of the river, I had a home also for some years in your town. Here I was ordained, and from here went to Turkey. My home in that country was first in old Pontus, near the locality where once it was supposed golden fleeces could be found; so far as my information goes, there are none there now. From Pontus I went to Capadocia, and from there to Constantinople in Ancient Thrace. Changing my home so often, when called upon to register my name, for instance at a hotel, I sometimes doubt how to fill out the blank for locality. Perhaps I may as well hereafter write West Springfield. Were this the time and place, I should be glad to give you some account of our mission work in Turkey. We are trying to establish there, these same institutions: schools, churches, which so bless West Springfield, and all New England, and the United States. And I should be glad if some of you could come out and see what measure of success we are having. It may be that some day, his majesty, the Sultan Abdulaziz, will call upon the people of his capital, Constantinople, to celebrate a centennial (I don't know whether it would be the twenty-second or the twenty-third centennial,) anniversary of the founding of the city; and I hereby avail myself of my privilege as a citizen for some years of that city, to invite any of you who will, to be present on that occasion when it occurs. Should any of you come there at any time, please follow the directions I will now give for finding there your West Springfield friends. Friends, I say, for my brother, Rev. I. G. Bliss, is also there, and he and his family are more of a West Springfield contribution to missions than I am, for although it did not occur to him any more than it did to me to be born here, he did what I did not, took his wife from one of your families, and they are both there still. When then you arrive in our harbor, and have somewhat satisfied yourselves by looking around upon the beautiful scenery, walk to the side of your steamer and call out "kaikjee." Soon a little boat will come along-side. Go down into it, but be careful to step into the middle of the boat lest you tip it over, and get a cold water bath. Say to the boatman, "Bagletché kapousé." When he brings you to a landing place, drop a shilling in the bottom of the boat and step out. As you enter the street passing by, turn to the right, go on till you come to Yene Jami mosque, pass through its court, then through Musir tcharshees, and keep up the street till you see written on a corner in Arabic letters, "Finjonjilee Sokak," turn that corner, and you will at once get sight of our Bible House, where you may be sure of a welcome from my brother or myself, or any one whom you may find there, and we shall be happy to show you our work and the city in which we live. That Bible House is an ornament and a blessing to Constantinople, and it is in a sort a West Springfield contribution to missions, for my brother has had a principal agency in collecting funds for it, and in its erection.

"*The Park Street Church*," was responded to by the pastor, REV. L. D. CALKINS:

MR. PRESIDENT AND FELLOW CITIZENS OF WEST SPRINGFIELD:—Though barely naturalized amongst you, and therefore inclined to remain a listener on such an occasion as this, I am, nevertheless inspired, by the theme proposed, to respond as well as may be to your call.

I have heard it said by naturalists that the descending axis of a plant, with all its rootlets and fibers is equal to the ascending axis with all its branches. In other words, that the entire root of a tree is equal to the entire body and branch. This being so it is true that in transplanting, except young and small growths, while we remove to the new place the entire body and branch, we always *leave behind* a considerable portion of the roots.

One of the earliest writers among the ancients, and who recorded his own interpretation of certain facts of nature; the movements of heavenly bodies, the flight of birds, the habits of wild beasts, said of plants; "There is hope of a tree if it be cut down, that it will sprout again, and that the tender branch thereof will not cease. Though the root thereof wax old in the earth, and the stock thereof die in the ground, yet through the scent of water it will bud, and bring forth boughs like a plant."

Well, sir, it happened in our town once, that there was a famous tree growing, whose seed had been planted a hundred and two years before, by the sainted John Woodbridge, on whose face we looked this morning in another room. It stood and it flourished in the midst of this Common, so near that its morning shadow must have reached to where you now sit, sir; and it was called, because of its comforting shade and healing leaves, the *Balm of Gilead tree.*

Three several gardeners, Woodbridge, Hopkins and Lathrop, watered and tended that tree, and dispensed its healing virtues to the honest people who rested beneath its shade, and together were encouraged to endure life's trials.

But now the time had come when the tree must be transplanted. It must be literally taken up from the valley to be set on the hill. It was a large tree, and an old tree, and required much care for such a change. So they dug deep, and they dug wide, and they enriched and watered well the new soil, and it struck root, grew, and spread itself yet more nobly than ever before, and it stands to-day a joy and a rejoicing to all who sit under its shelter and are nourished by its fruitage. But, sir, when that tree was moved the branches were wide and the roots both numerous and long, and some of these must needs be cut off and left to rot in the ground. But sir, they did *not rot!* or if they did it was only as the seed must first decay that the germ may burst forth, and after seventy-one years a shoot sprang from the ground, where the old rootlets hid themselves, as fair and fresh as if it were the first twig sprung from John Woodbridge's planting.

Mr. President, while we thank God for the old tree transplanted to yonder hill, let us also thank God for the old tree *blooming again* in the sprouting of its roots.

In conclusion let me humbly express my gratefulness to Him who has counted me worthy to water and tend this new tree sprung from that whose seed John Woodbridge sowed one hundred and seventy-six years ago. And let me also express the earnest and devout hope that it may always distill the same Balm of Gilead in which the forefathers took so much delight."

"*Agawam, the Second Daughter,*" was responded to by Mr. SAMUEL FLOWER, of Feeding Hills:

MR. PRESIDENT:—Had I supposed that I should be called without a moment's preparation to respond for "the youngest daughter" of this grand old town, I might wish that I could ask the privilege of the genuine son of the "Emerald Isle," who said that if he knew the time when and the place where he was to die, he should be a good way from it. And I am more embarrassed by the remark of my friend on my right, (Mr. S. L. Parsons,) that "Agawam was a prodigal, feeding upon husks."

While it is true that we cannot make so grand and imposing a show, nor aspire to so lofty pretensions as our elder sister, yet taking into account the fact, that we are almost entirely an agricultural population, we have advanced in material wealth, and in all the elements of prosperity, and of a healthy growth, to a degree of which we may be justly proud. In 1855, when Agawam was incorporated, we had a population scarcely exceeding one thousand, and a valuation of about half a million. Our valuation is now almost $1,200,000, and our population is between two and three thousand. And I hazard nothing in saying that a more prosperous, intelligent and law-abiding community cannot be found in the county of Hampden, or in the Commonwealth of Massachusetts. It is probable that I may state one fact in relation to that part of the town (Feeding Hills,) in which I reside, which cannot be said of any other locality containing an equal population, that there is not a place at which ardent spirits are sold. And we may point with pride to sons of Agawam, whose voices have been heard in both houses of Congress, and who are, and have been, ornaments to, and have risen to positions of enviable distinction in the legal and medical professions, and others who occupy the sacred desk.

And we may point to the descendants of her sons, who emigrated to other parts of the country, who stand in the front ranks of our teachers, and who have contributed in no small degree to the prosperity of our educational institutions, which are among the crowning glories of the age in which we live.

And in conclusion, I may say that we rejoice in the prosperity of our mother town, and hope that her future may be as prosperous and happy as the past has been good and great.

"*The Medical Profession*," was responded to by Dr. P. LeB. Stickney, of Springfield, who interspersed his speech with many rich anecdotes:

When West Springfield was separated from Springfield, Dr. John Van Horn, being located in that neighborhood as a medical practitioner, became, in point of time, the first physician of the new town. Dr. Van Horn was the son of Sumner Van Horn, and was born in that part of Springfield in 1726. He had the advantages of a collegiate education, graduating at Yale College in 1749, at the age of twenty-three. After attending the required course of medical lectures, he located in that part of his native town, where he continued to practice his profession for nearly sixty years, dying in 1805 at the age of seventy-nine. He had the reputation of being a skillful physician, and was undoubtedly as well educated as the advantages and opportunities of the times would admit. He was a scholarly man and fond of literary pursuits. He was prominent in public affairs, and was the first "Town Clerk" of the new town. In the later years of his life he became hypochondriacal, and imagined himself incapable of making any effort whatever, and consequently betook himself to his bed, where he remained for nearly four years under the care of a constant attendant.

Dr. Seth Lathrop was the son of the Rev. Dr. Lathrop, and was born in 1762 in that parish which was then a part of Springfield, and over which his father was pastor. He studied medicine with Dr. Van Horn, became his partner and afterwards succeeded him in his practice. Dr. Bronson, who knew him intimately, says of him, "He had a strong mind, sound judgment and excellent common sense; was frank, social, and fond of anecdote, and well read in the medical literature of the last half of the last century; an able and acceptable practitioner. More than six feet high, with a large frame, and straight, his figure was imposing, his very appearance inspiring in him a reliable confidence." He was very successful in his business, for his good, practical common sense supplied the want of an extended liberal education, and gave him a success which does not always accompany greater learning and accomplishments. He lived all his life in his native town, and was for many years engaged in his professional business. He suffered in the later part of his life from consumption which assumed an asthmatic form. He died in 1831, aged sixty-nine years.

Dr. Reuben Champion was the first physician who was born in the town of West Springfield. He was the second son of Reuben Champion, and was born in 1784, ten years after the town was separated from Springfield. His grandfather, Reuben Champion, M. D., having removed to Springfield from Saybrook, Ct., in the early part of the Revolutionary war, in order that his family might be in a more retired place and away from the liabilities of intrusion from the opposing military forces. He there located his family and entered the army as a surgeon, in which capacity he served with eminent success. He was with the army at Ticonderoga, where he died in 1777, being fifty years old. He left two sons, Reuben and Medes, both of these, although quite young men, served as soldiers in the army.

Dr. Reuben Champion received his early education at the academy in Westfield, and afterwards entered the office of Dr. Sumner of that town, with whom he began the study of his profession. He attended medical lectures at the medical school connected with Dartmouth College, which was then under the principal charge of the celebrated surgeon, Dr. Nathan Smith, who was the original founder of the school. During this time he was a private pupil of Dr. Smith, from whom he received more careful instruction respecting what was then termed the new method of treating and managing typhus fever; a method, which with few modifications, prevails at the present time. Having finished his course at the Dartmouth school, Dr. Champion attended a course of lectures in New York City, when returning to his native town, at the request of his fellow citizens, he there commenced the practice of medicine in 1809. With his new ideas of the treatment of typhoid fever, which he carried out notwithstanding the great opposition from both laity and the profession, he became quite successful in the treatment of the disease and gained an enviable reputation. He was an ardent Jeffersonian Democrat, and took an active part in local and general politics. He served the town in many public

10

offices, was Justice of the Peace, and represented his Senatorial District in the General Legislature. He was a member of the Massachusetts Medical Society, and continued in the practice of medicine for nearly fifty years and died in 1865, aged eighty-one.

Dr. Henry Bronson settled in West Springfield in 1827. Having passed through a thorough preparatory course of study he entered the Medical Institute of Yale College, receiving his medical degree in 1827. He remained in the town but a short time, removing to Albany in 1830. Possessing fine talents which had been carefully cultivated, with refined and gentlemanly manners, accompanied with a genial social character, and a mind well stored with general and professional knowledge, he rapidly gained a large share of practice. He was greatly beloved by many and had the respect and confidence of all.

Fond of literary and scientific pursuits, he devoted a large share of his spare time to these studies, in which he shortly gained an enviable reputation. In 1872 he was appointed Professor of Materia Medica in the Medical Institute of Yale College, a chair which he adorned and distinguished by his extensive and varied learning, and admirable style of lecturing. He resigned his professorship and the general practice of his profession in 1860, since which time he has been busily engaged in those more general and scientific studies to which he has been so long devoted.

Dr. Ebenezer Jones was born in West Springfield, and after preparing himself for the practice of medicine, settled in his native town. He remained there some twelve years, when he removed to the eastern part of the State.

Dr. Timothy Horton, whose father was a physician before him, was a practitioner of considerable ability, and had a good reputation as a physician and as a public man. Having sufficient means of living, he was noted for the extremely small charges for his medical services. His regular fee in his own immediate neighborhood was twelve and a half cents per visit, rarely ever charging over two shillings (33⅓ cents), no matter how difficult the case or the distance traveled. He was frequently known to go a distance of four or five miles, spend considerable time in holding a consultation with some brother doctor, and charging for his fee one shilling. He was a man of good sound judgment, and was much respected and esteemed by his fellow-citizens.

Dr. Dunham was a physician of good reputation, but of whom but little is known, having died some fifty years ago. He practiced in that part of the town known as Ireland Parish.

Dr. Calvin Wheeler settled in West Springfield, Feeding Hills parish. He was a surgeon in the army during the war of 1812 and in 1816. Although a man of limited education—like many others who at that time found it difficult to obtain the thorough knowledge of their profession which characterizes the progress of the present day—he gained by his strong mind and good judgment the confidence and respect of his patrons. He died in 1851.

Dr. Edwin McCrea practiced medicine for some twelve years in the town, in Agawam parish, settling there in 1832. His health was poor, which materially affected his ability to take care of his business. He was a good practitioner, and a genial and good-hearted man. He died in 1859.

Dr. Cyrus Bell settled in the parish of Feeding Hills in 1840. He graduated at the Berkshire Medical School in 1839, and soon after commenced the practice of his profession, locating himself in that part of the town in which he now resides, and which is now a part of the town of Agawam.

Dr. Sumner Ives was born in West Springfield, Ireland Parish. After obtaining a medical education, he located in this part of the town in 1826, remained there about five years and then moved to Suffield, Conn., and was there engaged in his profession as a successful practitioner until his death in 1845.

Dr. Solomon Chapman succeeded Dr. Ives in 1832; resided and practiced in that parish about ten years, then removed to Easthampton where he died.

Dr. Lawson Long succeeded Dr. Chapman in 1850. He still resides and practices his profession in the same parish, but which is now a part of the city of Holyoke.

Dr. Chauncy Belden was a graduate of the Yale Medical College in 1829. He was a private pupil of Dr. Woodward of Wethersfield, Conn. After graduating he served as an assistant in the Hartford Insane Retreat. He came to West Springfield in 1832, but left in 1842 and removed to South Hadley.

Dr. Belden suffered from ill-health for many years, finally dying of consumption in 1845. He was a well educated man and fond of scientific pursuits. In his practice he exhibited good judgment and skill, and was remarkably successful in the management of disease. He was greatly beloved by every one, gaining and retaining their confidence; he was kind and sympathetic in his nature and devotedly attentive to his patients.

Dr. Edward Strong, a native of Northampton, settled in West Springfield in 1839. He was a graduate of Williams College in 1834, and studied medicine at the Harvard Medical School in Boston, where he graduated in 1838. He continued to practice his profession until 1845, when, on account of ill-health, he relinquished it. Since then he has been engaged in the State department of "Vital Statistics," in Boston.

Dr. P. LeB. Stickney settled in West Springfield in 1845, graduated at Dartmouth College in 1839, and studied his profession at the Jefferson Medical College in Philadelphia where he graduated in 1842. He commenced the practice of medicine in that city, being connected with the Blockley Hospital as out-door physician and surgeon. Returning to his native State, he was induced to locate in this town where he remained six years, and afterwards removed to the city of Springfield where he now resides.

Dr. Nathaniel Downs, a graduate of the Harvard Medical School, settled in West Springfield in 1857. He remained but a few years and moved to Harvard in the eastern part of the State.

Dr. Edward G. Ufford settled in West Springfield in 1855. He gained a good practice and remained in the town till 1872, when, on account of ill-health, he removed to South Hadley and gave up the active duties of his profession.

Dr. Herbert C. Belden, son of Dr. Chauncy Belden, studied his profession in New York, graduating at the College of Physicians and Surgeons in 1867. He served a year as Assistant Surgeon in the Nursery Hospital, Randall's Island, N. Y., then went abroad, spending some time in study in Vienna, and returning home settled in West Springfield in 1871, where he now resides.

"*The Hill Meeting-House and its Founder, John Ashley*," was responded to by Rev. AARON M. COLTON, of East Hampton :

He said there it stands, and there it has stood for seventy-four years, in queenly beauty. Beautiful for situation—mountain of the Lord's house—whither the tribes go up.

It began with the century, and we trust will bless the century to its close. There eleven pastors, " elect, chosen of God, and precious," have sounded out the word of the Lord. " Their line is gone out through all the earth." And there two generations of the godly in Christ have worshipped, and waited for the consolation. That goodly house has breasted the storms of seventy-three winters. And strong as ever, foundation solid, timbers sound, spire erect, and " walls of strength embrace thee round." How many sermons in that house, how many prayers, how many songs, how many *conversions!* How many hearts and tongues have there been trained and tuned for worship in the temple not made with hands. Like its prototype in Jerusalem, it looks off on mountains round about. It has seen "fairy valleys rise," and villages blossom into cities, and the beautiful river, ever changing and still the same—a goodly scene—

> " Beneath, beyond, and stretching far away,
> From inland regions to the distant main."
> " Heavens ! what a goodly prospect spreads around."

That grand old house is a munition of rocks, fortress, citadel, watch-tower, sentinel, not frowning, but benignant, and saying, " All's well ! " Standing on that elevation, and crowning it, and looking off northward, eastward, southward, on a hundred thousand people, seen and seeing, and blessed by the vision, greeting all and severally " with an holy kiss." Itself pulpit, preacher, choir, song and benediction. " How amiable ! " How many hearts have warmed, how many eyes been filled with tears at beholding. How many souls from afar, have had longings to look upon it yet once more. What memories, sacred and precious, cluster around that house ! " " A thousand blessings on it rest ! " There the old meeting-house stands *to-day*, stately, grand, goodly, silent, eloquent, preaching righteousness, pleading for God and goodness, testifying the gospel of the grace of God. I beg you, sirs, not to claim for yourselves, of West Springfield, an exclusive proprietary interest in that house. No, sir, please. Not *yours* only, are the air and the sunshine, the stars, the trees, the streams. These are for all, and upon all—the common heritage. That house is for many, and me. If you built the house, you didn't the hill-top. "A city that is set on an hill cannot be hid."

But let me advert to an item of history. Having been a preacher in this valley for nearly thirty-four years, I have had scope for knowing something of the men who filled the pulpits here in an earlier time. Among them were *three* men, "in stature proudly eminent,"—excuse the "proudly"—Dr. Joseph Lyman, of Hatfield, Dr. Nathan Strong, of Hartford, and Dr. Lathrop, of West Springfield. Dr. Lyman, rigidly orthodox, cool, sagacious, born to command, learned, great in council. Dr. Strong—like his name—sound in doctrine, an able sermonizer, in style of writing clear and logical, in manner "decent, solemn, chaste," not a model of ministerial gravity in social intercourse.

Dr. Lathrop equalling the other two in their best qualities, and excelling them in easy natural grace, in suavity, in personal magnetism, with wonderful facility of adaptation to special occasions, not so strenuous upon extreme points of Calvinism, a bishop blameless, model of a man rounded out, complete—

> "Taken for all in all,
> "We ne'er shall see his like again."

And now *one more name* to be had in honor. A new meeting-house must be built. And where to be located? A vexed question—vexing a thousand parishes. So here; and thus a strife among brethren. Should the house be on the hill? The south side were not willing to go *up* the hill, and the north side were not willing to go *over* the hill. And the contention was sharp, and for a time threatened a rupture. And how was the difficulty adjusted? Happily the parish had a man of masterly wisdom and prudence in their pastor, Dr. Lathrop. A thought occurs to him. "The history of a thought is the history of a life." · So here, Dr. Lathrop has not the money, but he knows who has—a prince of a parishioner, John Ashley, Esq. The proposition is made, and is generously acceded to. Mr. Ashley will give the eminent domain, will contribute largely to the expense of building, and, in addition will endow the parish with a generous fund for the maintenance of the gospel. He comes forward with the offer, which is accepted—"So making peace." The meeting-house on the hill is thus *a peace-maker;* and with that sign it conquers. My apprehension is, that the hill-location was a pretty fair compromise, when considered in reference to the geography and population at that time. And then Mr. Ashley's grand donation for the *schools* of his town. Thus he idealized the great thought of the early Puritans and Pilgrims of New England—religion and education together—the meeting-house and the school-house side by side. Considering the times, those givings by Mr. Ashley were very liberal—princely. Those were not days of "shoddy" and stock-gambling. Men did not then *spring* to sudden riches. What was gained, was gotten by industry and prudence, by honest, patient, plodding toil. "The hand of the diligent maketh rich." All the greater and better the munificence in this case. The hundreds of thousands given in *our* day are not so much. All honor to the name and memory of John Ashley Esq.! Many among you, I am glad to know, still bear that name. May they all be worthy of it, and ever prove themselves worthy sons of worthy sires, by their liberal devisings for God's dear house and worship. The next time you pass along up Ashley street, look upon that very unpretending dwelling-house at your left on the hill. Not "an house of cedar" *that,* certainly. *There* lived and died John Ashley, "every inch a king," and of like zeal with Israel's king, for a dwelling-place for the most high.

I am so much of a stranger in your beautiful town, as not to know the spot where Mr. John Ashley was buried. From my distance I am fancying that grave to be on some sightly and sunny spot looking down on the Connecticut—your Thames. And to that hallowed shrine let many a pilgrim come, doing honor to the "dear parted shade" of one whose name is honorable, and should be had in everlasting remembrance. "Would you see my monument? look around!"

"Remembrance oft shall haunt the shore,
"When Thames in Summer wreaths is drest,
"And oft suspend the dashing oar,
"To bid his gentle spirit rest.

"And oft as ease and health retire
"To breezy lawn, or forest deep,
"The friend shall view *yon whitening* spire,
"And mid the varied landscape weep.

EXTRACTS FROM SPEECHES AND LETTERS.

ONE of the gems of the occasion was a sparkling little speech from Mr. CHAN LAISUN (of Springfield for the present, but really of Shanghae, China), in return to the toast, "*Our Chinese Cousins.*" He thanked the chairman for the honor, but he knew very little about West Springfield, and feared that a foreigner would make a mull of our affairs. In 1653, when this part of the State was peopled by those who came from England, religious liberty was in great agitation ; the house of Stuart was trying to subvert it, and, for that reason, these men fled from their comfortable homes. They planted then in the wilderness that old Bay tree, whose influence spreads east and west, and even far beyond the ocean. Hampden county, West Springfield—for the county is larger than the town, and in my land we always place the largest first,—the county of Hampden, you all know, was named after that great patriot, John Hampden ; and it has been the home of a spirit like his. I am happy to join with you in celebrating a hundred years, although in my own country I have often celebrated thousands. However, "despise not the day of small things." All matters must begin. The number one has to add the numbers two and three, and so on, to make the thousands. I am happy to thank Massachusetts in your persons. It was from a Massachusetts lady I first learned the English language ; and little then could I think to stand here to give Massachusetts thanks. One hundred years ago, the ocean-separated countries of Asia were almost totally unknown ; you knew not whether celestials or savages dwelt there. But now the children of China, the celestials, have taken umbrage under the shadow of kind Massachusetts.—There was no speech more entirely enjoyed than this.

"*The Memory of Dr. Joseph Lathrop*" was briefly replied to by his great-grandson, WILLIAM LATHROP, of Newton, Mass., who remarked that Rev. Dr. Vermilye had left him little to say in eulogy of his revered ancestor.

"*Holyoke the yearling city, although she takes a large proportion of water from the nursing bottle, she appears to be making a healthy growth,*" called up Alderman HENRY A. CHASE, who said that notwithstanding the unanimous acceptance of the centennial committee's invitation by his city government, no other member was at the banquet, and, like Job's servants after the calamity, he could say, "And I only am escaped alone to tell thee." Before taking his seat, he gave a finely condensed picture of Holyoke's present prosperous condition and habits, and excused the absence of Mayor Pearsons and his associates, who had pressing business engagements.

D. B. MONTAGUE, of Springfield, exhibited the identical square and hammer used by his grandfather, Capt. Timothy Billings, in building the First Church on the hill, and said, the contract price for that building was one thousand four hundred dollars, and ten gallons of St. Croix rum, valued at about sixty dollars. No rum was used, but the money was finally divided among the workmen. Six to ten hands were employed on the building, and the contractor thought he made about four dollars a day. The price of board was then from one dollar and twenty-five cents, to one dollar and fifty cents per week. The Parish Committee on building were Dr. Seth Lathrop, Justin Ely, Jr., Ruggles Kent and Moses Ashley. There was sharp competition for the job, and Capt. Billings, who was then only twenty-eight years old, was thought by some not to have beard enough for so large a work. He replied that "skill and courage were more necessary than beard." This hammer was forged by a common blacksmith, and this iron square, made in the same way, was the first used in this part of the country. All carpenters used for framing, prior to that period, was a scribe rule and a ten foot pole. The job was commenced in the spring of 1800, and the building dedicated June 24, 1802. The story is told, that when the steeple was complete, and the vane which resembles a sturgeon, adjusted, some waggish men assembled at the tavern of Mr. Rufus Colton, in Ramapogue street, got a rich treat out of the landlord. They told him they had made a bet for the drinks, etc., to be paid when the bet was decided. This was perfectly satisfactory, and after all had partaken and repartaken he was told that one party bet that when the church steeple fell, the vane would go to the north, and the other party that it would go to the south. Landlord Colton doubtless enjoyed the joke as much as his company, for he was a jovial man. The bet is still unpaid, and both landlord and abettors now sleep beneath the clods of the valley.

Dea. THOMAS TAYLOR, a wealthy farmer of Pittsfield, was another speaker. He said in substance: Mr. President, I left West Springfield in April, 1810, and found employment in the gun factory of Mr. Lemuel Pomeroy, of Pittsfield, at ten dollars per month and board. At the end of six months I took sixty dollars and a few clothes tied up in a handkerchief, and started on foot for my native town. I walked the entire distance, over forty miles, in a day, and handed over the money to my parents, reserving about twenty-five cents for my expenses back to Pittsfield. That was the way to make money once. My father and grandfather, natives of Tatham, both bore the name of Thomas Taylor. My mother was Clarissa Bagg, a daughter of Dea. John Bagg, and my love and recollections of her are now among the chiefest pleasures of my life. I was baptized by Dr. Lathrop at my father's house, the place now occupied by Mr. Elijah Sibley. My mother used to take me to church and place me on the pulpit stairs during service; whether because I was so good I am unable to say. This was in the old church, where over Dr. Lathrop's head and mine, was suspended that awful looking trap they called a sounding-board. Dr. Lathrop was very venerable in appearance, and the children were wont to form in lines on either side of the road as he passed, to do him reverence. With his hat turned up on three sides, he would bow in recognition, and after he had passed, those were the happiest who could say "he bowed to me."

The speeches did not close till night, nor did the throng disperse till the band were summoned to play the departing march, after which it was reluctantly moved and voted that "this meeting do now adjourn for one hundred years."

FROM A. A. WOOD, D. D.

LYONS, N. Y., FEB. 20, 1874.

MY DEAR MR. BAGG:—It would give me very great pleasure to be with you at the centennial celebration. But, as I have already written to you, this seems to be out of the question. I shall certainly be with you in thought and sympathy on that day, and I trust that the occasion will be everything that the most loyal child of West Springfield could desire. You will greatly miss some of the fathers of the town, who would have rejoiced had they lived to engage in such a commemorative service. Notably among these would have been Hon. Samuel Lathrop, and Sewell White, Esq. * * * * *

Sewell White, "Uncle Sewell" as we loved to call him, was a walking magazine of facts and incidents in regard to the early history of the town. He had some fact to state, or some quaint story to tell, in regard to almost all the old houses and families. I think of these in this connection, but there are many others whose names and faces rise before me—good men and true.

May the day be auspicious, and all the services everything that could be desired. With fragrant memories, and good wishes,

I am, my dear sir, yours most truly,

A. A. WOOD.

P. S.—My two West Springfield boys, are Edward A. Wood, Geneva, N. Y., and Wm. L. Wood, Indianapolis, Indiana.

FROM HENRY M. FIELD, D. D., OF THE NEW YORK EVANGELIST.

NEW YORK, March 20, 1874.

DEAR MR. BAGG:—It is a great temptation that you set before me in the prospect of your centennial celebration, and my heart's desire is to come to the feast; but the very day appointed for your village festival I am engaged here, so that I can only send you my best wishes for the blessed old town where we passed so many happy days. A place is always dear to us where we have been very happy; and the four years that I was your pastor form a bright and sunny chapter in my life. Was there ever a cosier shelter for a new-married couple than that modest parsonage under the trees, over which the great elms bent in loving protection? How often did we sit under their shade, book in hand, or talking with dear friends; or stroll along the banks of your beautiful river at twilight; or ride over the hills to hold meetings in the different districts of the town. It was then we tasted of your abundant hospitality. There is no fireside in the world more truly hospitable than that of a New England farmer, and when "the minister" comes nothing is too good for him. It seems to be Thanksgiving all the year round. Your people were indeed very, *very* kind to us, and their kindness will never be forgotten. Perhaps I fared better, coming after so many distinguished ministers, so that I inherited the traditional reverence. I have heard of troublesome parishes, and of crabbed old deacons, who vexed the life out of faithful ministers, but I know nothing of such from my own experience. The first man who received me at West Springfield was good Deacon Merrick, and it made me sad, as I rode by his house last summer, to think that he was gone, and that I should see his face no more. There too was Deacon Smith, who always came to meeting, rain or shine, and whose prayers were so simple and fervent they touched every heart; and many others whose faces rise before me as I write, whom you miss in your assemblies. They are laid to rest in the yard by the Common, or by the church on the hill, where "the forefathers of the hamlet sleep."

You meet to celebrate the completion of a hundred years! Where will you be a hundred years to come? Your children's children may live to see the day, but all who take part in this celebration will have passed from the earth. May it be that still, in that beautiful valley where it is your happiness to pass your lives, pleasant memories shall long linger among the trees, such as a good man could wish to leave behind. Few towns of New England have been favored with such a line of eminent preachers of the gospel. Remember their faithful teachings, and imitate their saintly examples; so, if you never see another such day on earth, you may celebrate your next centennial in heaven.

Very affectionately your friend, and the friend of everybody in West Springfield,

HENRY M. FIELD.

FROM T. H. HAWKS, D. D.

MARIETTA, O., MARCH 10, 1874.

MR. J. N. BAGG,—Dear Sir: It was a matter of great regret to me that I could not attend the centennial celebration of the incorporation of West Springfield on the 25th ult. I remembered with delight the centennial anniversary of Dr. Lathrop's settlement, observed the year after my installation, and would gladly have participated in the recent festival, expecting a similar occasion of pleasure.

But better motives influenced me. To have been with you would have been to mingle with dear friends, and revive precious memories of the days when our field of labor and our home were in the goodly old town. There for six years we experienced the greatest kindness, were associated with noble Christian workers both in the church and in sister churches, and reveled in scenes of natural beauty which have been a joy to us ever since we left the place. A minister may go far, but rarely will he find so many causes of happiness in his place of work as we had in West Springfield. I should like to pay a tribute of reverence and love, to some who were with us then, but who have entered into rest. I do not forget however, that your festival was commemorative of the incorporation of the town, and that such a tribute would rather befit a different occasion.

It is a peculiarity of New Englanders to love the places of their nativity with something of the warmth and devotion that characterize the Swiss and the Scotch. It is a work of filial love to gather together the fragments of history and put them in beautiful order, that as little as possible of the doings and sayings of their worthy ancestors may be lost. Their children will thank them for it, and so will some future historian.

West Springfield is fortunate in having one so able as Dr. Vermilye to put in permanent form some of the facts she would not have forgotten.

I feel much like a son writing of things that pertain to his mother and his childhood home; for if I was not "to the manor born," I claim the privileges of an adopted son. Let me now tell you in few words how it has fared with us since we left West Springfield in the Spring of 1861.

Our home was in Cleveland, till May, 1868. There two children were born to us; we had three when we went from you. By the goodness of God all are living. In June, 1869, we came to this place, where I am pastor of the First Congregational Church.

We have occasion to thank God for His leading. But in every place, and as long as we may live, we shall praise Him for giving us the privilege of living and working in the good old town whose natal day, a hundred years ago, has been so worthily commemorated, and it shall be our prayer that on her churches and on all her people the choicest blessings of heaven may be bestowed. Yours truly,

T. H. HAWKS.

LETTER FROM E. B. FOSTER, D. D.

LOWELL, MASS., March 23, 1874.

MY DEAR MR. BAGG:—Your programme of the celebration, and your very kind invitation to be present at the Centennial, came duly to hand. I wish, with great desire, that I could be in West Springfield to-morrow, to join in memories, prophecies, hopes, congratulations, thanksgivings. Hardly a field which the Lord has planted will give so many outlooks into the past and the future, which will be instructive, quickening and precious.

It is impossible for me to be present. My people meet to-night to consult with regard to some plan of rest, which they propose to give me. I am well-nigh worn out, and have asked for a vacation of six months, or for an associate pastor. A visit to your family, and to the dear churches, and to the town, would be a great joy to me; but I am too much exhausted, and too sensitive to exposures, to allow me to take any journey in these bleak March airs.

You ask for some particulars of my own history. I was born in Hanover, N. H., May 26, 1813. My father's name was Richard, my mother's Irene Burroughs. My maternal grandfather, Rev. Eden Burroughs, D. D., was for the first ten years of his ministerial life pastor of a Congregational church in Killingly, Conn., and for the last forty years of his life pastor of a Congregational church in Hanover, N. H. He was a life-long friend of President Wheelock, the founder of Dartmouth College, and for many years, as trustee and in the intimate fellowship of counsel, was associated with President Wheelock in the government of the college. I graduated at Dartmouth College in 1837; studied two years at Andover Theological Seminary; taught two years in academies in Pembroke, N. H., and Concord, N. H. I was married to Catherine, daughter of Deacon Orramel Pinneo, of Hanover, N. H., August 11, 1840. I was ordained pastor of the Congregational church, Henniker, N. H., August 17, 1841. I have also been settled as minister in Pelham, N. H., Lowell, Mass., and West Springfield, Mass. My eldest son, Addison Pinneo, now 32 years of age, is pastor of the Winnisimmet Congregational church in Chelsea, Mass. My eldest daughter, Emily, died aged 22, in West Springfield, Mass., Dec. 30, 1865, greatly beloved and greatly mourned. I have buried in their early childhood, just as the bud was beginning to break forth into mental and moral beauty, three sons—Charles, Edward and Bela. My youngest daughter, Nellie, is 17 years of age. I have published, on different subjects, twenty sermons and addresses. Through the gracious favor of a loving and guardian God, my pastorates have all been very happy, and I trust have not been without some fruits of blessing and of usefulness, in churches quickened and in souls converted.

Be assured, my dear Deacon Bagg, of my abiding gratitude to the dear old church of West Springfield, now working for Christ in two bands,—a living fountain from which richest streams of good have flowed. Be assured of the high honor and esteem in which I hold the men and women of the town, whose record has been one of integrity, enterprise, mental culture, generosity, noble progress. Be assured that my prayers will never cease for the large-minded and the large-hearted friends I found there, and for whose love and counsel I bless the Lord every day that I live.

With much love, and grateful remembrances to all,

Very affectionately yours,

EDEN B. FOSTER.

FROM REV. HENRY M. GROUT.

CONCORD, March 18, 1874.

J. N. BAGG, ESQ.—My Dear Sir: It is with unfeigned regret that I find myself unable to accept your kind invitation to be present at the approaching "Centennial" of your beautiful and famous town, and take some part in its exercises. I comfort myself, however, with the thought, that in so large and distinguished a company, my presence or absence could not much affect the interest of the occasion. A considerable portion of my last year at West Springfield was spent in looking up the early history of the Ancient Church upon the hill; so that, although the last and youngest of all the pastors who have gone out from you, I came to feel myself on quite familiar terms with the early settlers. It struck me curiously, in tracing and identifying some hundreds of names, that, with two or three exceptions if I rightly remember, double Christian names made their appearance upon the records after the beginning of the present century. It was somewhere about that time that plain, substantial John and Sarah began to give place to the more fanciful and sentimental John Henry and Sarah Jane. We are not sure that this indicates any radical change in the character of the people, but pass the fact over to those philosophically inclined, as one worthy of their attention.

Among other discoveries we fancied we made, in connection with our historical researches, was the apparent mistake of those who imagine that there has been a decline in the church-going habits of our old New England towns. Such certainly has not been the case in West Springfield. Remembering that there are not fewer than twenty churches within the bounds of what was once the solitary First Parish—of what a goodly family is she the yet vigorous mother;—it is evident that there at least, the excellent example of the fathers has not been forgotten. Then we observed, that, notwithstanding the frequent reduction of its families by the formation of new societies, each succeeding half-century has witnessed yet more numerous accessions to the original and mother church. Beginning with the year 1721, the first covered by existing records, three hundred and thirteen were added to its membership the first half-century, four hundred and forty-five the second, and six hundred and six the third. If, in these, and other respects, the course of improvement goes on in this way another half-century, so many of your scattered sons and daughters will desire to return to the delightful shade of your elms and maples, that there will be hardly room to receive them. I am with loyal spirit, and grateful memories, Very truly yours,

HENRY M. GROUT.

FROM DEA. ELISHA ELDRIDGE.

ANN ARBOR, March 12, 1874.

GENTLEMEN:—As I cannot be present at the centennial celebration on the 25th I will give you a few recollections.

My father moved into West Springfield from Berlin, Ct., in 1790, during my infancy. Ministers and meeting-houses occupied more attention formerly than at present, and hence these are among my earliest recollections. The first meeting-house was situated near the middle of the Town Common. It was a square building, with doors on three sides. It had three roofs or stories, each story being smaller than the one below it, and the highest came to a point surmounted by an iron rod, which supported a huge sheet-iron vane. The inside of the house was built mostly of oak timber, including the pulpit. On the right of the pulpit, in the gallery, the treble singers sat. Opposite were the bass singers, while directly in front of the pulpit, the tenor and counter were seated. There was one seat in the gallery above all the rest occupied by the gentry or aristocracy. Dea. Pelatiah Bliss led the singing for a number of years, and afterwards Hon. Samuel Lathrop. Rev. Dr. Joseph Lathrop was a large, portly, venerable looking man, who preached in the same pulpit over sixty-four years, and until Dr. Sprague's settlement.

I recollect looking up into the old pulpit one Sabbath morning and seeing a man that looked more like a straggler than a preacher. His hair looked as if it had not been combed for many days. This was Rev. Mr. Ballantine, of Westfield, who had made an exchange with Parson Lathrop. Timothy Billings, of Deerfield, contracted to build the meeting-house on the hill for one thousand four hundred dollars, and a suitable accompaniment of good rum. The raising took place while a vessel was building on the Common, and the men there employed, assisted in raising the steeple. * * * Yours truly,

ELISHA ELDRIDGE.

FROM ALONZO CHAPIN, M. D.

MANCHESTER, March, 24, 1874.

J. N. BAGG, Esq.—Dear Sir: I find myself, much to my regret, unable at the last, to be present at your centennial. I send my kind regards to all present, with the following sentiment: "Our Alma Mater. Other scenes and other cares may divert us, but our early love we do not forget."

I will at some time try to tell you, as requested, of the Chapin family.

Wishing you, as I have no doubt you will have, a very memorable occasion,

I am, yours truly,

A. Chapin.

FROM PROF. GEORGE E. DAY.

Yale College, March 24, 1874.

Gentlemen: Please accept my thanks for the invitation extended to me to attend the centennial celebration at West Springfield. It would give me great pleasure to be able to accept it, but other engagements prevent.

Although not a son, I can claim to be a grandson of West Springfield. There my ancestors have lived for many generations, and I shall always cherish a filial interest in all that concerns its prosperity.

It is not forgotten on this ground that one of your former pastors, the distinguished Dr. Lathrop, was called in 1793 to become Professor of Divinity in this College, and that the names of many natives of West Springfield appear upon its Triennial Catalogue.

In this list of graduates, the town is represented by two sons of the first minister, Rev. John Woodbridge, by his successor Rev. Samuel Hopkins and his son Samuel, by Dr. Lathrop who succeeded him and his son Hon. Samuel Lathrop, not to mention others among the living and the dead. May a true regard for education continue to characterize the town to the latest generation.

Respectfully yours,

George E. Day.

LETTER FROM N. T. LEONARD.

Westfield, April 18, 1874.

J. N. Bagg, Esq.—My Dear Sir: In accordance with your request that I should state the substance of my reminiscences in regard to the inhabitants of West Springfield, which the state of my health prevented my giving orally at the celebration, I would state: My father, Nathaniel Leonard, was a native of Sheffield; of which town his father, bearing the same name, was one of the original proprietors. His mother was Sarah Flower, sister of Col. Samuel Flower and Mr. Timothy Flower.

She died when my father was five years of age, and his father when he was but twelve. On the happening of the latter event, my father and one of his sisters were taken into the family of Major Jesse McIntire of Feeding Hills,—who was half brother of his father, and his wife's own sister of his mother,—where he remained from 1776 to about the time of the close of the Revolutionary war. Some incidents occurring during this time indicate the privations to which those living in that trying period voluntarily submitted, as well as their primitive modes of life.

Major McIntire had a good farm, and his house, which was the only one of brick in that era and vicinity, was some twenty feet square and a story-and-a-half in hight. This served the purpose for accommodation of at least six children, embracing the orphans and, it is my impression, Sarah [Ely], the grandmother of my father, her first husband being Nathaniel Leonard, and after his death (the fashion of dissolution by divorce not then being introduced) she intermarried with Mr. William McIntire. In this household the fare of the children was very plain. Sometimes when the pot had been boiled and the meat taken up, the liquor (thickened with flour or meal, the boiling process continued) served as one dish. At another time the liquor was made available by dipping bread into it and thus making toast. Bean porridge was another savory dish. The good aunt, of blessed memory, not only treated her orphaned sister's children as well as her own, but better; for while her boys sometimes refused the plain pies ordinarily prepared, when those of better flavor were served she was accustomed to give my father the largest piece, as a reward for having eaten what was set before him. He (Maj. McIntire) and his wife were accustomed to sit beside each other, and to eat from the same plate at the table.

The plains between Feeding Hills and Agawam furnished a supply of fat-pine stumps and knots, which served for light in the kitchen fire-place by which my father worked out his problems in arithmetic, and—under the instructions of his grandmother—acquired his mode of reading the Scriptures, which he followed in after life, in which the sound given to some of the verbs was as follows:—"shoold, shault, woold, coold," for the words—should, shalt, would, could.

As I understand, Major McIntire was not only a man of substance, but of prominent position. An anecdote which has recently come to my knowledge shows the estimation in which he was held as a reliable man.

A garrulous man having given a narration to a company when Rev. Dr. Lathrop happened to be present, and some incredulity being manifested at the recital, "It's true, every word of it," said the narrator; "I had it from Major McIntire." "Yes," replied Dr. L., "but we don't seem to have it direct from Mr. McIntire."

During a residence in Feeding Hills from 1824 to 1830, I made the acquaintance of a number of my kindred. Timothy Flower, a great-uncle and an esteemed member of the Baptist church, was a man of Zaccheus-like stature, though the fact of his encasing his nether limbs in long stockings and breeches buttoned at the knees, according to the fashion of his early days, perhaps gave one a more distinct impression of his diminutiveness. But he had a large heart, and his conscientious and persistent efforts to do justice to others would be well illustrated by an anecdote which I would like to relate, but for the possibility it might wound the feelings of some now living. His son Spencer was the leading man in the Methodist church, and was at times a member of the Board of Selectmen.

Another cousin of my father (his mother being a Flower) was Justin Granger. He had a great fondness for music, a pleasant voice, and was to some extent a composer. A piece written by him, called "Repentance," was sung by the choir in the church. Mr. Frederick Hazen, now of Springfield, was the leader, and I think might furnish a copy of the tune for publication.

At the period above mentioned the town was territorially divided into four parishes—the Central or First, Agawam, Ireland and Feeding Hills. Each of the latter had from two to three religious societies or churches organized, while the first had but one.

The executive department of the town was a pentarchy, uniting the offices of Selectmen, Assessors, and Overseers of the Poor. They were the representatives of the parishes, the first having two members of the Board. Two of my father's cousins were members of this organization. Timothy Horton (his mother was a Flower), whose residence was in Agawam, was called not only to attend to the duties of a medical practitioner in that town, but in all the surrounding towns, having the reputation of being skillful in the administration of remedies and independent in his opinions.

Alfred, son of Colonel Samuel Flower, has within a few months been "gathered to his fathers" at the ripe age of 93, after having served his generation faithfully as a deacon in the Congregational church in Feeding Hills, a captain in the militia, a magistrate, and a representative in the Legislature. There was an incident in my intercourse with him that served to show the importance of a temperance pledge and organization in its influence upon others. In 1827, being called with him and another gentleman to attend to some business occupying a day or more, after our labors were completed, and being at a hotel, by direction of the other gentleman "a mug of sling" was brought into the room, of which Mr. F. declined partaking, stating that he had discontinued its use for some months; which was unknown to us, though in habit of almost daily intercourse. On the formation of a temperance organization, a few months after, he was of course ready to sign the pledge.

James Kent and Captain Hosea Day, who with his company marched to the defence of Boston in 1812 with Aaron Bagg and Luke Parsons, were associated with Messrs. Horton and Flower in caring for the interests of the town. They were accustomed to meet for the transaction of public business at landlord Colton's hotel,—a man who, notwithstanding the trials incident to his position, was recognized as a very devout person.

The Board audited all the bills, and were never suspected of anything like Tweedism or Mobilierism; and, avoiding even the appearance of evil, at the annual town meeting they were accustomed to make their bills for services at $1.00 per day, without charging for horse hire, and present them for allowance to the town, together with a bill of Mr. Colton's. On one occasion, the Moderator stating the question in regard to the latter, "Will the Town allow Mr. Colton's bill of $— for refreshments furnished the Selectmen," a voter, not accustomed to join in the discussions, occasioned a good deal of mirth by rising and, in a feminine voice, throwing his head back and looking at the presiding officer from under his glasses, saying—"Mr. Moderator, won't you please to read the items?"

I recall pleasant recollections of my acquaintance with the Elys,—Justin, Homer and Cotton of the first parish, Robert of the second, and Henry of the third.

I recollect the former saying to me in my bachelor days, "Mr. L., I think you would enjoy life much better if you were married." I pass the statement along to the young men of the present day, with the assurance that to me it has been doubly verified. Whether any of these were of my remote kindred by reason of my being descended from an Ely, or not, I cannot say. As to my kindred bearing my own name, I knew Justin, Phineas and Dwight, father and son; Elias, grandfather of Col. Parsons; Rufus and Asaph, the latter having, even in old age, an enthusiastic fondness for seine-fishing; Reuben and his son Robert, and their neighbors Apollos and William, all residents of Feeding Hills, and Thaddeus of Agawam, who married a sister of my father. None of these gentlemen were descended from any ancestor of mine nearer than Benjamin, who was the son of John, the first of whose fourteen children was born in Springfield in 1641.

An anecdote was related to me in regard to one of our name who was not then living, but with whose family I was intimately acquainted: A neighbor applied to him for a horse to make a journey. He made no direct reply. Three or four days after, meeting the applicant, he said—"HORSE! Yes; I don't care if you take him." To which the reply was—"Mr. Leonard, I have been to Hartford, and got back last night."

Perhaps it might be inferred from this that the operations of our minds, as a family, were rather sluggish.

THE CHURCH ON MEETING-HOUSE HILL,

ERECTED A. D. 1800.

APPENDIX.

The following is a literal copy of the record by which West Springfield first became a parish:

At a Great and General Court or Assembly for his Majesties Province of the Massachusetts Bay in New England, begun and held at Boston upon Wednesday ye 27th of May, 1696, In the Eighth year of his Majesties Reign, and Continued by Several Adjournments unto Wednesday the 18th of Novemb^{r} following.

Upon reading the petition of the Inhabitants of the Town of Springfield on the West Side of the great River running throug^{h} the s^{d} Town, Commonly called Connecticut River, therein setting forth their distance from the place of meeting for the publick worship of God in s^{d} Town, and the difficulties and danger attending their passing of the s^{d} River, besides many other inconveniences they lye under by reason thereof, being about Thirty-two Families and in number upwards of Two Hundred Souls, Praying that they may be Permitted to invite and settle a minister on that side of the River, that themselves and Families may enjoy the Ordinances of Christ and their Children not be in danger of becoming heathens for want of Instruction. And a Committee appointed by this Court of indifferent and Judicious persons belonging to the several neighboring Towns to inquire into that matter, having given a Meeting to the Inhabitants of the s^{d} Town and heard what was offered on both sides, Reporting that they judge the desire of the Petitioners to be reasonable, and that the granting of their Petition will not only promote Religion, but be much also for the worldly advantage of the Town.

Ordered, That the s^{d} Petitioners be, and hereby are, permitted, and allowed, to invite, procure and settle, a learned and orthodox Minister on the West side of the s^{d} River, to dispense the word of God unto those that dwell there, and that they be a distinct and separate Precinct for that purpose, the River to be the dividing Line. And that the Present Inhabitants on the west side of the s^{d} River, together with such as shall from time to time settle among them, have liberty to convene together, to advise, agree upon, and take such methods, as may be suitable and convenient, for the procuring, encouraging, settling and support of a minister qualified as afores^{d}, and for the building of a Meeting House according as shall be determined by a Major Vote, and also to nominate and appoint a Committee of three or more persons among themselves to transact and manage that affair. And all the Inhabitants and Estates under their Improvement lying on the west side of the s^{d} River shall stand Charged towards the settlement and support of the ministry in s^{d} place, in manner as the Law relating to the maintenance and support of the ministers does direct, and Provide, and be assessed thereto proportionably by two or more assessors as shall from time to time be Elected and appointed by the Major part of the s^{d} inhabitants for that purpose, who may also nominate and appoint a Collector, to gather and pay on the same as by Warrant or order under the hands of such Assessors he shall be directed, and when and so soon as the Inhabitants of s^{d} Precinct shall have procured a learned and orthodox Minister to preach the Word of God among them, they shall be freed and Exempt^{d} from paying towards the support of the Ministry on the other side of the River, and for so long a time as they shall Continue to have and enjoy such a Minister.

I consent
WM. STOUGHTON.

By order of the Lieutenant-Governour,
Council and Assembly.
Js^{A} Addington, Secr^{ty}.

A true Copy, Extracted from the Original.
Test. Nath^{L} Atchinson, Cler. for the Second Parish or Precinct in Springfield.

In April, 1707, the land on the west bank of the river was divided into plots of ten acres each, which were assigned by lot, to the male inhabitants of the town who had completed their twenty-first year. Their number was seventy-three, as shown by the following list, copied literally from the earliest records of the parish.

Jose Ely, Snr ,	Benja Lenord,
Jose Ely, Junr ,	John Day,
Wm. Macrany,	Jno. Lenord,
Jams Barcker,	Jams Tailer, Snr.,
Jose Barcker,	Jams Tailer, Junr.,
Sam'l Barcker,	Jonath Tailer,
Oliver Barcker,	Sam'l Tailer,
John Bag,	Edward Foster,
Jonathan Bag,	John Miller,

Nath'l Morgan,	James Mireck,
Sam'l Miler, Snr.,	John Killam, Snr.,
Sam'l Frost,	John Killam, Junr.,
Nath'l Sykes,	Benja Smith,
Pela Jones,	Wm. Smith,
John Peley,	Jose Lenord, Snr.
Sam'l Wariner,	Sam'l Lenord,
Eben'r Day,	Jose Lenord, Junr.,
Christian Vanhorn,	Sam'l Cooper,
Charls Fery,	Sam'l Kent,
Sam'l Day,	Gersham Hail, Snr.,
Sam'l Ely,	Jno. Hail,
Jno. Fowler,	Gersham Hail, Junr.,
Mr. Woodbridg,	Deacon Barber,
Eben'r Miller,	Thos. Barber,
Joseph Bodortha, Snr.,	Nat Bancraft,
Sam'l Bodortha, Snr.,	Jose Hodg,
Sam'l Bodortha, Junr.,	Isaack Frost,
Eben'r Jones, Snr.,	Jams Stevenson, Snr.,
Eben'r Jones, Junr.,	Jams Stevenson, Junr.,
Josiah Lenord,	Jona Worthington,
Lest Ball,	Sam'l Miller, Junr.,
Sam'l Ball,	Thomas Macrany,
Henry Rogers,	Joseph Bodortha, Junr.,
John Rogers.	Francis Ball,
Nath'l Dumbleton,	John Ely,
Wm. Scot,	Sam'l Fery.

[See Historical and Genealogical Register of Boston, October number, 1874, for a literal transcript of twenty pages of Parish Records, descriptive of the manner in which the land was divided among the settlers in West Springfield, in 1807–20.]

PETITION OF THE PARISH TO BE SET OFF AS A TOWN IN 1756.

" At a Meeting of the Inhabitants of the Second Parish in Springfield, July 15, 1756, Capt. Benj. Day, Moderator, voted 1st, To Chuse a Committe to prefer a Petition to the Great and General Court of the Massachusetts Bay, That they would set off all the Inhabitants and the Lands on the West Side the Great River in Springfield, To be a Distinct Town with all Priviledges belonging Thereto.

Voted 2ly, That Capt. Benj. Day, Doct. John Vanhorne, Capt. Joseph Miller and Mr. Josiah Day be a Committe for that purpose."

ACT OF INCORPORATION, FEB., 1774.

" *Anno Regni, Regis, Georgia, Tertia, Decimo, Quarto.*"

An Act for dividing the Township of Springfield and erecting the Western Part thereof into a Seperate Town by the Name of West Springfield passed Feb., Anno Domini 1774. Whereas, by Reason of the great Extent of the Township of Springfield, the Remote Settlements, Disputes, Controversies and different Interests of the Inhabitants thereof, the Difficulty and often Impractibility of the Assembly in Town Meetings for Elections and other necessary purposes by Reason of the Great River Connecticut, almost equally dissecting the Township, it is necessary that there be a Division thereof.

Be it enacted by the Governor, Council and House of Representatives. That that Part of the Township of Springfield lying on the West Side of Connecticut River, and the Inhabitants thereof be constituted and erected into a different Town by the Name of West Springfield, and be invested with all the Powers, Privileges and Immunities which by the Laws of this Province, Towns have and enjoy. Provided, &c.

FIRST WARRANT FOR TOWN MEETING.

Hampshire, SS. To the Constable or Constables of the Town of Springfield, or either of them Greeting.

You are hereby required in his Majesties Name forthwith to warn and give notice to the Freeholders and other Inhabitants on the West Side of Connecticut River in West Springfield, that they meet and assemble together at the Old Meeting House in said Town on Wednesday the 23d Day of this Instant at Ten of the Clock in the forenoon then and there to act on the following articles.

1st. To choose a Moderator in Said Meeting.

2d. To choose Town Officers in s'd Town for the year ensuing.

3d. To See if the Inhabitants will apply to the General Court for any alteration in the incorporating act, as was made the last seting of said Court that incorporated the Inhabitants on the West Side the River, in s'd Town into a Seperate Town.

4th. To give Liberty for Swine to go at large being yoked and ringed.

5th. To choose a Commitee to hire Bulls for the Town's use.

6th. To bring in the votes for a County Treasurer. Hereof, fail not, but make due Return of this Warrant, with your Doings thereon unto us the Subscribers, or to the Clerk of s'd Town, at or before the Time set for s'd Meeting, given under our Hands and Seals the 14th day of March, in the 14th year of His Majesties Rein, Anno Domini 1774.

Benjamin Day, Charles Pynchon, Nathan'l Ely, 2d, Aaron Colton, John Hale, Jonath White, Benjamin Ely, Selectmen of Springfield.

SOME OF THE TOWN'S OFFICERS WITH THEIR YEAR OF SERVICE.

MODERATORS.

Col. Benjamin Day, 1774–79, 81–85, 87–89.
Dn. Jona White, 1774–79, 81–84, 86, 87.
Abram Burbank, 1775, 76, 78, 80, 81, 86.
Justin Ely, 1775, 76, 84, 87, 90, 92–99, 1801.
Maj. and Col. Benjamin Ely, 1778–80, 81, 83, 86, 96.
Doct John Vanhorn, 1780, 85, 86, 88, 90.
Capt. Levi Ely, 1780.
Eliphalet Leonard, 1783, 87, 89, 91.
Capt. John Williston, 1783, 91, 1800.
Deac. Jacob Winchell, 1787.
Dea., Capt. and Col. Pelatiah Bliss, 1788, 90, 92, 93, 95–97, 99.
Doct Seth Lathrop, 1789, 93, 1800, 1, 7.
Horace White, 1789.
Martin Ely, 1789.
Elias Leonard, 1792.
John Ashley, 1793.
Jonathan Smith, Jr., 1794, 98–1819.
Capt. Joseph Morgan, 1799.
Lucas Morgan, 1800.
Joseph White, 1801.
Heman Day, 1802, 5, 6, 22, 26, 32.
Pliny White, 1804, 5
Maj. Roger Cooley, 1804.
Maj. Gad Warriner, 1806.
Aaron Bagg, 1811.
Col. Aaron Bagg, 1841, 42, 52–67, 70, 72, 74.
Hon. Samuel Lathrop, 1811, 22, 27, 30, 32, 34, 37, 38.
Doct. Timothy Horton, 1811, 18.
Charles Ball, 1814.
Luke Parsons, 1819–28.
James Kent, 1820, 21, 26, 29–31, 33.
Alfred Flower, 1828, 29, 41.
Norman T. Leonard, 1830.
Reuben Champion, 1832, 43, 44, 49.
Amos Worthington, 1833.
Linus Bagg, 1834–36.

Caleb Rice, 1838.
Lyman Whitman, 1839–41.
Lester Williams, 1844, 71.
Daniel G. White, 1845, 46, 48, 49–54, 56–58.
Josiah Johnson, 1845.
Edward Parsons, 1845, 59, 66, 73.
Cyrus Frink, 1845–47.
Newbury Norton, 1848.
Augustine Ludington, 1848.
Martin King, 1849.
J. W. Freeland, 1853.
Orson Swetland, 1855.
Reuben Palmer, 1855.
Aaron Ashley, 1857, 58.
Samuel Smith, 1859.
Ocran Dickinson, 1860.
Amzi Allen, 1861.
Andrew Bartholomew, 1864, 65, 68, 69, 72–74.
Ashbel Frost, 1864.
D. F. Melcher, 1865.
William Smith, 1866.
Isaac B. Lowell, 1867.
Norman T. Smith, 1869, 72.
Reuben Brooks, 1869.
Ethan Brooks, 1870, 71, 74.
Henry A. Sibley, 1870, 72, 73.
J. L. Worthy, 1871.
Harvey D. Bagg, 1871.
C. W. Hoisington, 1871.
Amos Russell, 1872.

CLERKS AND TREASURERS.

(Where two names occur in one year the last named is Treasurer.)

Doct. John Van Horne, 1774.
Doct. Chauncey Brewer, 1775–80.
Justin Ely, 1781.
Aaron White, 1782–95.
Joseph White, 1782–95.
Aaron White, 1793–95.
Horace White, 1793–95.
Samuel Lathrop, 1796–98.
Horace White, 1796–98.
Seth Lathrop, 1799.

Horace White, 1779.
Aaron White, 1800–12.
Heman Day, 1800–12.
Reuben Champion, Jr., 1813-21.
James Kent, 1813–21.
Caleb Rice, 1822–34.
James Kent, 1822–34.
Charles Ely served as Treasurer part of 1834.
Reuben Champion, Jr., 1835-42.
Lester Williams, 1835–42.
Michael Marsh, 1843–47.
Lester Williams, 1843–47.
Edwin F. Perkins, Clerk, pro tempore.
Enoch N. Smith, 1848.
Harvey Bliss, 1848.
Enoch N. Smith, 1849.
Lester Williams, 1849.
Enoch N. Smith, 1850–53.
Charles White, 1854, 56–62.
Lewis Leonard, 1855.
Edward Parsons, 1863.
John M. Harmon, 1864–74.

REPRESENTATIVES.

(At first only persons with an income of forty shillings, or of forty pounds sterling, were allowed to vote for Representative.)

Col. Benjamin Day, 1774, 78.
Maj. and Col. Benjamin Ely, 1775, 78–80, 82, 85, 88, 89.
Dea. Jonathan White, 1776, 77, 79, 87.
Mr. and Esq. Justin Ely, 1777, 80–85, 90–97.
Mr. Eliphalet Leonard, 1777.
Abraham Burbank, Esq., 1780, 81, 83, 84.
Capt. John Williston, 1786–89.
Mr., Esq. and Hon. Jonathan Smith, Jr., 1794–96, 98–1811, 14–19.
Mr. Jere Stebbins, 1804, 8.
Mr. Heman Day, 1805.
Maj. Gad Warriner, 1805, 9, 14, 15.
Col. Samuel Flower, 1806, 10.
Lieut. Charles Ball, 1806, 08, 09, 11, 12, 15, 16, 20, 27.
Doct. Timothy Horton, 1807, 10, 11.
Mr. Luke Parsons, 1807, 10, 13, 14, 22, 23.
Maj. Jesse McIntire, 1808.
Mr. Elias Leonard, 1809, 11, 13.

Capt. John Porter, 1812, 13.
Mr. James Kent, 1812, 13, 27.
Mr. Horace Flower, 1812.
Col. David Morley, 1814.
Capt. Alfred Flower, 1815, 16, 23, 26, 27.
David Hastings, 1816.
Caleb Rice, 1821, 24–26, 28.
Daniel Merrick, 1823.
Jona E. Ferre, 1823.
Luther Frink, 1824, 36.
John Street, 1827.
Norman Warriner, 1827.
Doct. Reuben Champion, Jr., 1829, 35.
Robert Ely, 1829.
Warren Chapin, 1829, 31.
Spencer Flower, 1829, 39.
Lewis Warriner, 1830, 31, 33, 36.
Henry Ely, 1830, 33.
Capt and Maj. Linus Bagg, 1831, 32, 36.
Capt. Henry Phelon, 1831, 32.
Asa B. Whitman, 1832.
Capt. Hosea Day, 1833, 34.
Josiah Johnson, 1833, 36, 38.
Benjamin Leonard. 1834.
Seth Parsons, 1834.
Heber Miller, 1834.
Samuel Noble, 1835, 37.
Dwight Leonard, 1835.
Amasa Ainsworth, 1835.
Pelatiah Ely, 1837.
Edwin H. Ball, 1838.
Lester Williams, 1839, 40, 49, 69.
Lyman Whitman, 1839.
Rufus S. Payne, 1840.
Ebenezer B. Pelton, 1841.
Col. Aaron Bagg, 1842, 71.
Lucien M. Ufford, 1842.
Asa Clark, 1843.
Isaac Roberts, 1843.
Edward Parsons, 1846.
Harvey Chapin, 1846.
Daniel G. White, 1848, 50.
Lyman Allen, 1848.

Wells Southworth, 1849.
Harvey Wolcott, 1851.
Edward Southworth, 1852, 53.
Samuel D. Warriner, 1854.
Jonathan W. Freeland, 1855.
Jonathan O. Moseley, 1856.
George L. Wright, 1858.
Nathan Loomis, 1860, 63.
Justin L. Worthy, 1865.
Charles A. Fox, 1867.
William Melcher, 1868.
George C. S. Southworth, 1870.
Ansel H. Ward, 1871.

DELEGATES TO PROVINCIAL CONGRESS AT WATERTOWN, MASS.

Dea Jona. White, Doct. Chancey Brewer, Maj. Benj. Ely, 1775.

DELEGATES TO CONSTITUTIONAL CONVENTION.

Abraham Burbank, Maj. Benj. Ely, 1780.
Col. Benj. Ely, Capt. John Williston, 1787.
James Kent, Timothy Horton, Luther Frink, Alfred Flower, 1820.
Homer Ely, 1853.

DELEGATES TO CONVENTION AT HATFIELD, FOR REDRESS OF GRIEVANCES.

Col. Benj. Ely, Capt. John Williston, 1782.
Eleazer Day, Joseph Selden, 1783.
Col. Benj. Ely, 1786.

SELECTMEN.

Col. Benj Day, 1774, 79, 81, 84.
Dea. Jona. White, 1774, 79, 82.
Col. Benj. Ely, 1774, 75, 78, 79, 82, 84, 86,88, 94.
Dea. John Leonard, 1774, 75.
Lt. Benj. Leonard, 1774, 75.
Doct Chauncy Brewer, 1775.
Justin Ely, 1775.
Dea. Reuben Leonard, 1776–79,
Lt. and Capt. Joseph Morgan, 1776, 87, 95–99.
Eliphalet Leonard, 1776, 77, 81, 83–87.
Charles Ball, 1777.
Abraham Burbank, 1778–82, 85, 86.
Benj. Stebbins, 1780–87.
Capt. Levi Ely, 1780.
Lt. Enoch Cooper, 1780–82.
Capt. Joseph Ely, 1780, 81.

Aaron White, 1781.
Capt. John Williston, 1783–97.
Russel Leonard, 1783, 87.
Lucius Morgan, 1783.
Joseph White, 1788, 92.
Samuel Phelps, 1788, 96.
Reuben Leonard, Jr., 1788–97.
Heman Day, 1793–98, 1800–6.
Maj. Gad Warriner, 1797–99.
Lt. Ruggles Kent, 1798, 99.
Elias Leonard, 1798, 99, 1809, 11, 12, 15–17.
Horace White, 1799.
Justin Granger, 1799.
Lt. Benj. Ashley, 1800, 1.
Robert Ely, 1800–7.
Doct. Timothy Horton, 1800–24.
Justin Leonard, 1800, 1.
Pliny White, 1803–7.
Col. Sam'l Flower, 1802, 3.
Maj. and Col. David Morley, 1804–8.
Jonathan Smith, Jr., Esq., 1807–13.
Luke Parsons, 1808–10, 16–27.
Aaron Bagg, 1808–21, 23, 24.
Col. Aaron Bagg, 1837–44, 48, 54, 56, 57, 63.
Luther Frink, 1811–13.
Horace Flower, 1813, 14.
James Kent, 1814–21, 23–25, 31, 32.
Peres Hitchcock, 1814, 15.
Alfred Flower, 1818–26.
Ruggles Kent, 1822.
Jonathan Parsons 1822.
David Hastings, 1825, 26.
Hosea Day, 1825–29.
Caleb Rice, 1826–30.
Spencer Flower, 1827–30, 34, 35, 42, 43.
Lewis Warriner, 1827–29.
Warren Chapin, 1828, 29.
Linus Bagg, 1830–36.
Benj. Leonard, 1830–33.
Henry Ely, 1830–32, 35, 36.
Josiah Johnson, 1831–33, 37, 38, 44.
Charles Ball, Jr., 1833, 34.
Edward Parsons, 1833, 35, 45–57, 60.

Samuel Noble, 1834–37.
Lester Williams, 1836–44.
Silas Dewey, 1836–44.
Willard Ely, 1837–41.
Lyman Whitman, 1838, 39–42.
Calvin Wheeler, 1839.
Ebenezer B. Pelton, 1840.
Cyrus Frink, 1842, 43, 48.
Newbury Norton, 1843, 45–47.
Asa Clark, 1844.
Lucien M. Ufford, 1844.
Isaac Roberts, 1845–47.
Russell Gilmore, 1845–47.
Homer Ely, 1845–47.
Augustine Ludington, 1848.
Herrick Brooks, 1848.
Wm. S. Bowe, 1848, 51–54.
Enoch Leonard, 1848.
Nehemiah D. Perry, 1848.
Sam'l Flower, 1848.
Harvey Bliss, 1848.
Lester Hamlin, 1849, 54.
Ralph Adams, 1849.
Jona. O. Mosely, 1849–53, 56, 57.
Harvey Chapin, 1849.
Daniel G. White, 1849–53.
Jona. W. Freeland, 1850–53.
Sam'l Smith, 1851–53, 55.
L. S. Brown, 1854.
George B. Bebee, 1854.
S. L. Griggs, 1855.
Orson Swetland, 1855.
James T. Smith, 1855.
Orrin Root, 1855.
James P. Ely, 1856, 57, 60.
S. B. Day, 1858–60.
Riley Smith, 1858–60.
Daniel Ashley, 1858–60.
Nathan Loomis, 1861, 62.
Alvin Sibley, 1861, 62, 74.
Frank F. Smith, 1861, 62.
Charles C. Smith, 1863.
Lucius Dwinnell, 1863.

Albert D. Bagg, 1864–66.
C. W. Hoisington, 1864, 65.
Aaron L. Hayes, 1864–67.
William Smith, 1866, 67.
Harvey D. Bagg, 1867–74.
Charles White, 1868, 69.
Henry A. Sibley, 1868–73.
Amos Russell, 1870–74.

SCHOOL COMMITTEE.

Rev. Reuben S. Hazen, 1827–32, 34, 35, 37, 88.
Dr. G. White, 1827–30, 35, 36, 38.
Sam'l Lathrop, 1827–29.
Henry Ely, 1828, 30.
Horace Palmer, 1827, 28.
Thos. Barrett, 1827, 29.
Rev. Wm. B. Sprague, 1827.
Rev. Thos. Rand, 1827.
Justin Ely, 1829.
Hezekiah Griswold, 1830, 33.
Dr. Reuben Champion, 1830, 31.
Norman T. Leonard, 1829, 30.
Solomon Lathrop, 1830, 32–35.
Rev. Thos. E. Vermilye, 1831-34.
Rev. Hervey Smith, 1831–38.
Rev. Henry Archibald, 1831, 32.
Rev. John W. McDonald, 1833.
Rev. Horatio J. Lombard, 1834, 35.
Rev. John H. Hunter, 1836.
Rev. Jona. L. Pomeroy, 1836.
Rev. P. Brockett, 1836.
Elisha Eldridge, 1837.
Aaron Day, 1837, 38.
Rev. Calvin Foote, 1837, 38.
Rev. A. A. Wood, 1839, 41–45.
Doct. Reuben Champion, 1839, 46–48.
Rev Hervey Smith, 1839.
William Taylor, 1839.
Palmer Gallup, 1839–43.
Aaron Bagg, 1840.
Horace D. Doolittle, 1840, 41.
William Gamwell, 1842.
Rev. William L. Brown, 1843, 45.

Rev. Gideon Dana, 1844.
Rev. Dillon Williams, 1844, 45.
Rev. Lester Lewis, 1846.
Rev. Thomas Rand, 1846, 47.
Josiah Johnson, 1847, 48.
Rev. Ralph Perry, 1848–55.
Rev. Simeon Miller, 1848.
Daniel G. White, 1848, 56.
Rev. Asahel Chapin, 1848, 49.
Doct. P. LeB. Stickney, 1849–51.
Rev. Henry M. Field, 1852.
Doct. Cyrus Bell, 1851–53.
Doct. Nathaniel Downes, 1853, 56, 57.
Rev. Henry Cooley, 1854.
Rev. S. D. Ward, 1854, 55.
Rev. Theron H. Hawks, 1855–59.
Rev. E. Scott, 1855.
S. D Warriner, 1855.
Lewis H. Taylor, 1855.
E. Clark, 1855.
Amzi Allen, 1857, 60–62.
John B. Taylor, 1858.
Riley Smith, 1858.
J. N. Bagg, 1860, 61, 69, 70, 72, 73.
Nathan Loomis, 1861–63.
Rev. Eden B. Foster, D. D., 1862–64.
Rev. Henry M. Powers, 1862–65.
Daniel F. Melcher, 1864, 65, 69.
Ethan Brooks, 1864–67, 71.
Rev. Moody Harrington, 1864.
Rev. J. S. Batchelder, 1865, 66.
Rev. Perkins K. Clark, 1866–68.
Daniel F. Morrill, 1866–69.
Norman T. Smith, 1868–70, 72–74.
Dr. Herbert C. Belden, 1870.
Emerson Geer, 1871–74.
Gideon Wells, 1871.
Sarah Isabel Cooley, 1872–74.
Angeline Brooks, 1872.
Charles E. Merrick, 1872–74.

POSTMASTERS IN WEST SPRINGFIELD CENTER.

Since the organization of the Department, unless some were entered previously in the Post-office books destroyed by fire.

NAME.	DATE OF COMMENCEMENT.
Jerre Stebbins,	18th Dec., 1802.
Benj. Stebbins,	19th Feb., 1817.
Miner Stebbins,	26th Oct., 1819.
Elias Winchell,	27th Aug., 1824
Henry Cooley,	16th Nov., 1836.
Edward Southworth,	30th Sept., 1841.
M. M. Tallmadge,	9th May, 1845.
Michael Marsh,	29th Apr., 1846.
Lester Williams,	31st Aug., 1847.
P. LeB. Stickney,	5th June, 1849.
Lewis Leonard,	2d June, 1851.
W. E. Cooley,	24th July, 1866.
Henry A. Phelon,	13th Feb., 1867.

THE BAGG PEDIGREE.

[Condensed from a "Genealogy of the Bagg Family in America," now in process of compilation by Lyman H. Bagg (187). Of the numbers to which the star (*) is attached additional information is desired.]

JOHN BAGG, supposed to have emigrated from Plymouth, England, died at Springfield, Sept. 5, 1683. In 1660 he conveyed lands in the "second division," probably on the west bank of the river, to Hugh Dudley, of Chicopee Plains; in 1668, his name was signed fourth to a petition against imposts; in 1678, Jan. 1, he was one of the citizens to whom Major John Pynchon administered the oath of allegiance. He married Oct. 24, 1657, HANNAH BURT (b. April 28, 1641, d. Aug. 1, 1680), dau. of Deacon Henry Burt and Ulalia his wife, who emigrated from England to Roseburg, and thence removed to Springfield in 1640.

Their children were: 1, Hannah, b. 1658, d. 1740, m. 1681, Nathaniel Sikes. 2, Mercy, b. 1660, d. 1738, m. 1679, Ebenezer Jones. 3, Daniel, b. Nov. d. Dec. 1663. 4, JOHN, b. March 26, 1665, d. Nov. 1740, m. March 30, 1689, MERCY THOMAS (b. May 15, 1671), *and had eleven children, from three of whom all the Baggs now living in West Springfield are descended.* *5, Daniel, b. 1668, d. 1738, m. 1694, Hannah ——, and had ten children, from two of whom descended the Baggs of Westfield, Lanesboro, Pittsfield, Utica, Detroit, Montreal, and Northern New York. 6, Jonathan, b. 1670, d. 1746, m. 1696, Mary Weller (d. 1740), and had nine children. *7, Abigail, b. April 23, 1673, fate unknown. 8, James, b. 1675, d. 1689. 9, Sarah, b. 1678, m. 1701, Benoni Atchison (d. 1704); m. 1711, Samuel Barnard. *10, Abilene, b. July 25, 1680, fate unknown.

Second Generation. Children of 4 John: *11, Mercy, b. March 6, 1690, fate unknown. 12, Hannah, b. 1692, d. 1764, m. 1715, Daniel White. 13, Sarah, b. 1694, d. 1726 (?), m. 1717, Samuel Taylor. 14, JOHN, b. April 23, 1696, d. Jan. 28, 1776, m. Jan. 7, 1730, ELIZABETH STOCKWELL (d. June 11, 1792, a. 88), and had five or more children. 15, Abigail, b. 1699, m. 1724, John Day. 16, James, b. 1702, d. 1749, m. 1744, Bathsheba Dewey, and had three children. 17, Thankful, b. 1704, d. 1747, m. 1727, Joseph Leonard. 18, Rachel, b. and d. 1706. 19, Rachel, b. 1708, m. 1731, Pelatiah Morgan (d. 1741); m. 1750, Ebenezer Day, Jr. 20, THOMAS, b. Feb. 22, 1710, d. April 11, 1776, m. July 29, 1748, MARGARET ROOT (b. Nov. 21, 1716, d. Oct. 4, 1775), and had five children. 21, EBENEZER, b. May 14, 1713, d. March 18, 1803, m. July 21, 1748, LOIS LAMB (b. Nov. 13, 1720, d. June 2, 1793), and had five children.

Children of 6 Jonathan: 22, Mary, b. 1697, d. 1740, unm. 23, Jonathan, b. March 18, 1699, d. Oct. 7, 1746, supposed to have been unmarried. 24, Hannah, b. 1701, d. 1735, unm. (?) 25, Ebenezer, b. Feb. 14, 1703, m. July 18, 1754, Patience Killum, and had one son. 26, Elizabeth, b. 1704, m. 1748, Joseph Leonard. 27, Abigail, b. 1706, d. 1756, m. 1729, Benoni Jones. 28, Experience, b. 1708, d. 1748, m. 1747, John Ely. 29, David, b. Sept. 3, 1710, d. May 18, 1760, m. Oct. 21, 1736,

Hannah Stockwell (d. Jan. 29, 1789, a. 80), and had six children. *30, Mercy, b. 1712, d. 1746, unm. (?)

In the division of West Springfield land into ten-acre lots, among the 73 residents who were 21 years old and upwards, April 7, 1707, John Bagg (4) drew lot No. 9, and Jonathan (6) lot No. 13 in "Chickebey Field above Dorbeys Brook." Thirteen years later, John 14 and Jonathan 23, who were of the 44 young men who had attained their majority in the interval, drew lots near their fathers in the same field.

Third Generation. Children of 14 John: 31, John, b. Oct. 8, 1730, d. June 13, 1809, m. June 19, 1755, Rebecca Phelps (b. Dec. 10, 1737, d. April 18, 1797), and had nine children. 32, Elizabeth, b. 1732, d. 1823, unm. 33, Aaron, b. Oct. 8, 1736, killed in the battle at Lake George, Sept. 8, 1755. 34, Sarah, b. 1738, m. 1777, Israel Brooks. *35, Ebenezer, b. 1740, d. May 18, 1796, a. 56, m. 1772 (?) Orpha Granger, and had eight children.

Children of 20 Thomas: 36, Thomas, b. Aug. 10, 1749, d. March 27, 1837, m. Dec. 18, 1777, Joanna Cooley (d. Jan. 9, 1787, in her 34th year); m. May (?), 1788, Eunice Sackett (d. Aug. 14, 1819, in her 65th year), and had nine children. 37, Israel, b. April 16, 1752, d. July 10, 1838, m. Jan. 11, 1776, Sarah Green (d. Jan. 10, 1832, a. 78), and had eight children. [This family moved to Bernardston, where most of their descendants have since resided, and the present record will not trace them further. All the eight children attained to extreme age, and four were still living in April of the present year, to celebrate the 97th birthday of the eldest, Israel, who was born at W. S. April 14, 1777, and is the longest-lived person known to this genealogy.] 38, Oliver, b. Jan. 27, 1754, d. Nov 17, 1833, m. Aug. (?) 1783, Tryphena Day (d. Aug. 25, 1803, a. 51); m. Feb. 5, 1807, Jerusha Ely Taylor (d. Feb, 2, 1836, a. 73), and had three daughters. 39, Ezekiel, b. 1756, d. 1758. 40, Margaret, b. 1758, m. 1778, Jephtha Green. 41, Ezekiel, b. Jan. 24, 1761, d. Jan. 1, 1837, m. Jan. 4, 1787, Huldah Cooley (d. July 17, 1833), and had five children.

Children of 21 Ebenezer: 42, Thankful, b. 1749, d. 1818, m. 1778, Noadiah Loomis. 43, Frederick, b. Nov. 18, 1750, d. Nov 15, 1823, m. May 28, 1772, Chloe Taylor (d. Dec. 15, 1818, a. 66), and had eleven children. 44, Warham, b. Nov. 1, 1752, d. Sept. 14, 1803, m. Sept. 30, 1773, Sarah Ashley (d. Sept. 27, 1805, a. 52), and had five children. *45, Walter, b. Nov. 9, 1754, m. June 17, 1779, Nancy Granger, and had five children. 46, Judah, b. April 2, 1758, d. Aug. 18, 1812, m. Oct. 31, 1780, Anna Roberts, and had four children.

Child of 25 Ebenezer: 47, Ebenezer, b. July 27, 1756, d. April 24, 1759.

Children of 29 David: 48, David, b. 1737, d. 1756. 48½, Hannah, b. 1739, d. 1757, m. 1756, Ebenezer Miller, 3d. 49, Noah, b. 1740, d. 1746. 50, Abigail, d. Dec. 15, 1759, a. 16. 5, Mercy, b. 1746, d. 1768, m. 1764, Stephen Ward. 52, Mary, b. 1748, m. 1766, Stephen Morgan.

Fourth Generation. Children of 31 John: 53, Clara, b. 1756, d. 1765. 54, Aaron, b. Sept. 23, 1757, d. Aug. 16, 1839, m. Sept. 27, 1775, Sarah Miller (d. Sept. 7, 1829, a. 69), and had five or more children. *55, Chloe, b. 1760, d. 1797, m. 1785, Ithamar Morgan. *56, Charlotte, b. 1763, m. 1785, Elijah Bliss. 57, Clarissa, b. 1766, d. 1837, m. 1787, Thomas Taylor. *58, Sophia, b. 1769, m. 1787, Stephen Day. 59, Orrel, b. 1774, d. 1826, unm. *60, Helen, b. 1776, m. 1796, Reuel Vanhorn. *61, Mary Meekins, b. 1779, m. 1804, Theodore Cooley.

Children of 35 Ebenezer: 62, Ebenezer, b. Feb. 8, 1773, d. April 27, 1817, m. Feb. 5, 1801, Lucy Cooley (d. July 17, 1843), and had three children. 63, James, b. 1774, d. 1795, unm. 64, Pliny, b. March 24, 1776, d. Sept. 9, 1863, m. May 31, 1810, Sabra Nelson (b. April 7, 1787, d. May 14, 1849), and had six children. *65, Heman, b. March 24, 1776, d. about 1840, unm. 66, Elizabeth, b. 1777, d. 1810, m. 1796, David Wilder; m. 1810, James Bagg. *67, Orpha, m. 1800, Solomon Dewey.

68, Abraham, b. Nov. 3, 1783, d. Sept. 5. 1867, m. 1810, Sophia Ashley (b. July 24, 1779, and had five children. *69, Mercy, d. 1860, m. 1806, Chester Smith; m. 1819, Daniel Noble.

Children of 36 Thomas: 70, Thomas, b. Dec. 10, 1778, d. about 1840, m. Nov. 12, 1807, Lauretta Hosford, (b. May, 1782, d. April, 29, 1846), and had four children. *71, Joanna, b. 1781, m. 1799, John Gaylord. 72, Justin, b. 1782, d. 1786. 73, Huldah, b. 1725, d. 1857, m. 1806, Linus Fowler 74, Eunice, b. 1782, d. 1803. 75, Justin, b. March, d. Dec. 1792. 76, Justin, b. Dec. 13, 1793, d. Feb. 5, 1861, m. 1817, Frances Sackett (d. May, 1, 1860, a. 74), and had four children. 77, Nancy, b. 1796, d. 1803. 78, Clarissa, b. 1798, m. 1818, Jeffrey Seymour.

Children of 38 Oliver. 79, Tryphena, b 1789, d. 1867, m. 1815, Elisha Eldridge. 80, Amanda, b. 1793, d. 1872, unm. 81, Grata, b. 1795, d. 1864, m. 1818, Horace Smith.

Children of 39 Ezekiel: 82, Ezekiel, b. Jan. 16, 1788, d. Oct. 17, 1825, unm. 83, Richard, b. Nov. 22, 1789, d. Jan. 4, 1860, m. Jan 3, 1809, Flavia Rogers (b. Jan. 15, 1789, d. Feb. 15, 1870), and had four children. 84, Huldah, b. 1791, d. 1801. 85, Justus, b. July 5, 1795, d. March 15, 1871, m. 1826, Sarah Munn Day (d. Jan. 26, 1839, a. 38); m. 1839, Delia Loomis (b. Dec. 29, 1818), and had six children. 86, Persis, b. 1798, d. 1803. 87, Mary, b. 1802, d. 1860, m. 1822, Hosea Bliss.

Children of 43 Frederick: 88, Chloe, b. 1774, d. 1794, m. Cyrus Starkweather. 89, Lydia, b. 1775, d. 1815, unm. 90, Frederick, b. 1779, d. 1800, unm. 91, Linus, b. Jan. d. March, 1780. 92, Malah, b. and d. 1781. 93, Malah, b. 1783, d. 1810, m. 1801, Francis Miller. 94, Tirzah, b. 1785, d. 1849, m. 1823, Hosea Bliss. 95, Linus, b. Sept. 8, 1787, d. Dec. 25, 1836, m. Jan. 14, 1813, Fanny Clapp (b. Nov. 25, 1790, d. Nov. 7, 1870), and had six children. *96, Hiram, b. 1789 (?), m. Aug. (?) 1824, Eunice Smith, and had one daughter. *97, Miranda, b. 1791 (?), m. Dec. 3, 1819, Amos Allen. 98, Henry, b. 1796, d. 1800.

Children of 44 Warham: 99, Lucinda, b. 1774, m. 1798, Joseph Button. 100, Sally, b. 1776, d. 1780. 101, Electa, b. 1778, m. William Alley. 102, Sally, b. 1780, m. 1803, Oliver Bemont. 103, Louisa, b. 1783, d. 1860, m. 1806, Rodney Day. 104, Miriam Porter, b. 1786, d. 1834, unm. 105, Celina, b. 1789, m. 1810, Simon Pitt Button.

Children of 45 Walter: 106, Daniel Granger, b. April 23, 1780, fate unknown. 107, Henry, b. 1781, d. 1786. 108, Jeremiah, b. 1785, d. 1799. 109, Fanny, b. 1787, m. 1813, George Lee Bow. 110, Walter, b. 1798, d. 1820, unm.

Children of 46 Judah: 111, Altamira, b. 1781, d. 1812, m. 1807, Horatio Kent. 112, Laura, b. 1783, m. 1831, Henry Lassells. 113, Judah, d. Aug. 1, 1812, a. 27, unm. 114, Zebina, b. Jan. 5, 1788, d. Nov., 1869, m. March 1828, Elinor Colton (b. April 5, 1802), and had five children. 115, Anne, b. 1800, m. 1826, Chandler Todd.

Fifth Generation. Children of 54 Aaron: 116, Nancy, b. 1776, d. 1829, m. 1796, Clark Loomis, 117, Annah, b. 1778, d. 1807, m. 1802, Joshua Street. 118, John, b. Sept, 29, 1780, d. Oct. 26, 1820, m. 1805, Sophronia Woodruff (d. Nov. 26, 1843, a. 55), and had eight children. 119, Lucy, b. 1782, d. 1873, unm. *120, Laura, b. 1785, m 1807, Joshua Street.

Children of 62 Ebenezer: *121, James, b. 1802, m. May (?) 1826, Maria S. Cochran (b. Oct. 28, 1804, d. June 24, 1835), and had two children. 122, Cooley, b. 1804, d. 1812. *123, Betsey, d 1830, m. 1824, Elias C. Taylor. *124, Orpha, b. 1807, m. 1824, Charles Williston. *125, Nancy, b. 1809. 126, Lucy, b. 1812, d. 1817. *127, Olive, m. Jacob Perkins.

Children of 64 Pliny: 128, Emily, b. 1812, m. 1834, Franklin Bliss. 129, Nelson Pliny, b. Sept. 12, 1814, d. Feb. 28, 1851, m. May 5, 1849, Julia Sophia House (b.

1831), had no children. 130, Ralph Merry, b. Oct. 3, 1817, m. Oct. 9, 1842, Lurania Bates Tiffany (b. July 8, 1817), and had one daughter. 131, Jemima Bond, b. 1820. m. 1843, Dwight Abner Perkins. 132, Ebenezer, b. April 9, 1823, m. May 22, 1846, Theda Miner Barnes (b. May 5, 1824), and had two children. 133, Orpha Lurania, b. 1825, m. 1845, William Henry Barnes.

Children of 68 Abraham: 134, Henry Granger, b. 1811, d. 1829. 135, Mercy, b. 1813, m. 1840, Nathaniel W. Osborn. 136, Charles Francis, b. March 9, 1815, m. 1842, Catherine Bliss (b. Sept. 2. 1822), and had four children. 137, Susan Miller, b. 1821, m. 1844. Hervey H. Phettiplace. *138, Henry Granger, b. April 10, 1831, three times married, but without children, his first wife was Frances Lincoln (d. June, 1860, a. 25).

Children of 70 Thomas: *139, Sylvester, b. Oct. 31, 1808, d. about 1858, unm. *140, Lewis Hosford, b. Aug. 15, 1810, m. about 1832, Lucy Maynard (d. before 1840), and had two sons. 141, Nancy Cooley, b. 1812, m. 1835, James Loomis.

Children of 76 Justin: 142, Amarilla, b. 1816, m. 1842. George H. Chapman. 143. Justin Dwight, b. 1818, d. 1836. 144, Seymour, b. April 7, 1820, m. Jan. 25, 1855, Elizabeth Nancy Gassett (b. Sept. 12, 1833), and had one daughter. 145, Franklin Sackett, b. Feb. 9, 1826, m. June 10, 1872, Ellen Louise Ashley (b. June 13, 1834).

Children of 83 Richard: 146, Harriet Maria, b. 1810, d. 1872, m. 1831, Henry Parsons. 147, Richard, b. March 20, 1812, d. Oct. 29, 1852, m. Jan. 3, 1838, Nancy Bliss (b. June 12, 1814, d. Dec. 21, 1838); m. Jan. 3, 1841, Susan Atwater (b. July 14, 1817), and had three children. 148, Mary, b. 1817, m. 1837, Edward Joseph Bull. 149, Flavia Jane, b. 1822, m, 1851, Henry A. Marsh.

Children of 85 Justus: 150 Justus, b. 1829, d. 1830. 151, Harvey Day, b. March 16, 1831, m. March 2, 1856, Clymena Ashley (b. Oct. 15, 1827), and had one son. 152, William Gilbert, b. Feb. 4, 1833, m. Feb. 4, 1858, Persis Ely Brooks (b. Feb. 13, 1833), and had six children. 153, Sarah Winnifred, b. March, d. June, 1838. 154, Huldah Maria, b. 1840, m. 1866, Henry L. Ashley. 155, Joseph Loomis, b. Oct. 3, 1843, unm.

Children of 95 Linus: *156, Frederick Henry, b. Dec. 6, 1813, d. March 14, 1867, m. April (?) 1839, Eunice Avery, and had four children. 157, Peres Munn, b. Nov. 23, 1815, m. Jan. 30, 1840, Sarepta Gamwell (b. Jan. 17, 1821), and had six children. 158, Joseph Strong, b. Sept. 8, 1818, d. June 9, 1859, m. Oct. 29, 1853, Aurelia Brown (b. July 29, 1820), and had two sons. 159, Albert Dwight, b. June 30, 1821, d. May 30, 1874, m. May 25, 1843, Julia Bagg Button, (d. Jan. 24, 1846, a. 25), m. Feb., 1850, Harriet S. Otis (d. Oct. 3, 1850, a. 30), m. Jan. 22, 1852, Harriet Atherton Sibley (b. Sept. 22, 1829), and had three sons. 160, Fanny Clapp, b. 1823, d. 1824. 161, Fanny Clapp, b. 1826, d. 1871, m. 1851, Henry A. Pratt.

Child of 96 Hiram: *162, Henrietta, m. 1850, J. Francis Downing.

Children of 114 Zebina: 163, Rufus, b. Feb. 22, 1830, lost at sea. 164, Anne, b. Feb. 22, 1830, unm. 165, Edward, b March 19, 1836, m. Sept. 20, 1868, Eliza Noxon (b 1843), and had two children.

Sixth Generation. Children of 118 John: 166, Sophronia, b. 1806, m. 1825, Edward Parsons. *167, Annah, b. 1807, d. 1846, m. 1828, Abraham Dwight Miller. 168, Aaron, b. 1808, d. 1809. 169, Aaron, b. Feb. 6, 1810, m. Nov. 17, 1834, Hannah Mather (b. Sept. 12, 1819, d Sept. 5, 1836), m. Oct. 16, 1837, Lucy Maria Mather (b. June 5, 1820), and had six children. 170, Sarah Miller, b. 1812, d. 1844, unm. 171, John, b. March 13, 1814, d. March 1, 1850, m. Elvira Brown and had two daughters. 172, Sullivan, b. 1817, d. May 17, 1845, m. Sept. 15, 1841, Cordelia M. Williams (d. April 4, 1847, a. 25), and had one son. 173, Lucy Jane, b. 1820, d. 1844, m. 1841, Samuel Dale.

Children of 121 James: *174, James. *175, Annette.

Child of 130 Ralph Merry: 176, Jane Elizabeth, b. July 14, 1843.

Children of 132 Ebenezer: 177, Nelson Edward, b. Feb. 28, d. Sept. 18, 1860. 177½, Carrie Etta, b. Dec 28, 1851.

Children of 136 Charles Francis: 178, Charles Henry, b. April 27, 1843, m. Nov. 14, 1866, Mary Louise Harmon (b. April 17, 1847), and had two children. 179, Ella Catherine, b. 1845, m. 1865, Wallace Grow. 180, Adalaide Augusta, b. 1849, m. 1868, Edward M. French. 181, Frank Bliss, b. July 28, 1858.

Children of 140 Lewis Hosford: 182, Edward, b. about 1834. 183, son, name unknown, b. about 1836.

Child of 144 Seymour: 184, Frances Elizabeth, b. Jan. 1, 1856.

Children of 147 Richard: 185, Nancy Elizabeth Bliss, b. 1838, m. 1861, Frank H. Fuller. 186, Richard Atwater, b. Nov. 29, 1843, m. Oct. 17, 1866, Martina Sanchez Doringh (b. Sept. 12, 1848), and had three daughters. 187, Lyman Hotchkiss, b. Dec. 24, 1846.

Child of 151 Harvey Day: 188, William Harvey, b. April 27, 1857.

Children of 152 William Gilbert: 189, Frank Parmelee, b. April, 1863. 190, Arthur, b. Feb. 26, 1865. 191, Charles Philo, b. April 4, 1867. 192, Harry, b. June 19, 1870. 193, Harriet, b. Jan. 13, 1872. 193½, daughter, b. May, 18, 1874.

Children of 156 Frederick Henry: *194, Chloe, m. John Lovekin. *195 Frederick. *196, Malah, m. Charles Cogswell. *197, Emma, m. Clarence Bailey.

Children of 157 Peres Munn: 198, Linus Lester, b. May 19, 1841, m. Jan. 12, 1869, Julia A. Woodward (b. Jan. 4, 1840), and had two children. 199, Celia Fanny b. Nov. 23, 1842. 200, Homer Dwight, b. Jan. 18, 1846, m. April 14, 1869, Maria Raymond (b. Nov. 14, 1848, d. Aug. 3, 1872), and had one son. 201, Ella Sarepta, b. 1849, m. 1867, Thomas P. Mather. 202, Caroline Amanda, b. July 15, 1856. 203, Harriet Cora, b. Sept. 28, 1858.

Children of 158 Joseph Strong: 204, William Joseph Strong, b. July 6, 1854. 205, Joseph Linus, b. 1857, d. 1858.

Children of 159 Albert Dwight: 206, Frank Albert, b. Jan. 27, 1853. 207, Atherton Sibley, b. Aug. 18, 1856. 208, Edgar Lavant, b. Aug. 4, 1859.

Children of 165 Edward: 209, Anne Gertrude, b. May 27, 1870. 210, George Edward, b. Aug. 10 (?), 1871.

Seventh Generation. Children of 169 Aaron: 211, Hannah Mather, b. 1836, m. 1856, Ethan Brooks. 212, Aaron, b. June 21, 1839, m. June 9, 1869, Mary Heath, (b. March 5, 1845), and had one daughter. 213, Lucy Maria, b. June 26, 1842. 214, Rufus Mather, b. Dec. 20, 1844, m. Dec. 20, 1865, Mary E. Bartholomew, and had four children. 215, John Sullivan, b. Dec. 31, 1848, m. May 30, 1872, Louise E. Shivelin (b. Feb. 22, 1853), and had one dau. 216, Edward Parsons, b. Aug. 28, 1855.

Children of 171 John: 217, Elvira, b. 1840, m. 1861, m. George Wright. 218, Helen M., m. 1868, Joseph F. Griggs.

Child of 172 Sullivan: 219 Sullivan, d. Nov. 8, 1865, a. 22, unm.

Children of 178 Charles Henry: 220, Helen Fuller, b. March 21, 1868. 221, Daisy Maud, b. Nov. 7, 1869.

Children of 186 Richard Atwater: 222, Susan Sanchez, b. July 17, 1867. 223, Martina Doringh, b. Jan. 8, 1869. 224, Louise Atwater, b. March 2, 1874.

Children of 198 Linus Lester: 225, Harrison Lester, b. Nov. 29, 1869. 226, Frederick Arthur, b. Feb. 17, 1871.

Child of 200 Homer Dwight: 227, Edward Dauso (?), b. April 13, 1872.

Eighth Generation. Child of 212 Aaron: 228, Clara Edith, b. Oct. 16, 1871.

Children of 214 Rufus Mather: 229, Laura Street, b. March 15, 1867. 230, Rufus Mather, b. April 19, 1869. 231, Edward Oren, b. May (?) 1871.

15

Child of 215 John Sullivan: 232, Louise Elinora, b. May 25, 1873.

Of the following Baggs, supposed to belong to the pedigree, the proper places therein have not yet been discovered. Any information in regard to them, or in regard to the numbers marked with a star (*), will be thankfully received by the compiler.

Abigail, d. Dec. 5, 1759. Thankful, m. Jan. 1768, Nathaniel Gaylord, of South Hadley. Martha, m. Dec. 17, 1787, William Alley (or Ashley). Lucinda, d. July 22, 1821, a. 57, m. April 13, 1791, Enoch Deane, and had a dau., Hadassah Bartlett, d. Sept. 20, 1800. Mercy, m. Aug. (?), 1791, Amos Green, of Sharon, Vt. Mercy, m. Sept. 27, 1797, Lemuel Felt. Naomi, baptized July 3, 1768. Chester, b. April 14, 1772. Sarah, b. June 30, 1774.

GENEALOGY OF THE ASHLEY FAMILY.

Benjamin Ashley died may 11, 1772, 75; his wife died December 25, 1788, 87; their children were Moses, drowned in the great pond, July 27, 1792, 61; Aaron died suddenly October 29, 1799, 71; Mary (Taylor) died June 9, 1809, 82; David died March 28, 1813, 78; John died July 17, 1824, 84; Benjamin died June 19, 1828, 91.

From Moses descended Elisha and Moses.

Aaron and John were childless.

From David descended David, Jr., Solomon, Noah, Justin, Enoch and Aaron, also Lucretia, wife of Genubath Bliss, and Eunice, wife of Eli Ashley.

From Benjamin descended Benjamin, Jr., and Elijah.

Probably the first record of the Ashleys is in the following memorandum:

"March 13, 1660—61.

There is grant[d] to Rob[t] Ashley, six acres of Meadow on the back side of Chicopee Plain, within 2 or 3 Mile of the Great River, where he Can find so much Undisposed of.

A Copy from Springf'[d] Records, exa[d] by Wm. Pynchon, Clerk.

GENEALOGY OF THE CHAMPION FAMILY.

Reuben Champion and Lydia Duncan, his wife, came to West Springfield, as a place of refuge for his family, from Saybrook, Ct., in the beginning of the Revolutionary war. He was in the army as surgeon, and died of fever at Ticonderoga, N. Y., in 1777, aged 50. He left four daughters, and two sons, Reuben and Medes.

Reuben Champion, Jr., born 1760, died 1832; married Silence Ely, and had issue: Harvey, Reuben, Lovicy, Elias, Moses and Aaron, twins, Henry, John, Silence, Francis, Flavia, Maria.

Harvey settled in Westfield, was a farmer, and died in 1860.

Reuben Champion, 3d, born 1784, died 1865; married Pama Stebbins; was a physician and farmer, and had issue: Elizabeth, married Paoli Lathrop, of South Hadley; Franklin, died 1861.

Elias was a hatter by trade, and died in 1839.

Moses died, 1838.

Aaron is a merchant, and resides in Savannah, Ga.

Henry died, 1829.

John died, 1845.

Silence married Col. David Moseley of Westfield.

Flavia and Maria reside on the old Amostown homestead with their nephew James, son of Elias.

GENEALOGY OF THE CHAPIN FAMILY.

Moses A. Chapin, familiarly known as "Saddler Chapin," from his occupation, was also a well-to-do farmer, near the old toll-bridge. He was born in Somers, Ct., in 1762, settled in West Springfield in 1777, married Lucina Graves of Hatfield in 1787, had ten children, six of them sons, and died in 1841. His wife died in 1851, aged 85. Their children follow:

Mary, the eldest, married Avery Herrick, a farmer of Worthington, and had nine children. She died in Westfield in 1863, aged 75.

Moses, born 1791, graduated at Yale, studied law in Albany, settled in Rochester, N. Y., held the office of judge, was a prominent Presbyterian elder, had six children, and died in 1865. His eldest daughter, Maria, married Rev. Eli Smith of the Syrian Mission, and died in Beirut in 1842.

Augustus Lyman, born 1795, graduated at Yale, studied theology at Princeton, N. J., married in 1831, had four children, has preached in various places in the State of New York, and now lives with his daughter in Galesburg, Ill. His son, Lyman, is a missionary of the A. B. C. F. M. in Northern China.

Alpha, born in 1796, married in 1831, had three children, settled on a farm in Ogden, N. Y., was a Presbyterian elder, and died in 1868, aged 71.

Seth, born in 1800, was a commission merchant in New York city, and died unmarried in 1833.

Elizabeth, born in 1802, married H. M. Ward of Rochester, N. Y., had four children, and now lives with a daughter in De Soto, Mo. Her son, Henry A., has been Professor of Natural History in Rochester University.

Alonzo, born 1805, graduated at Amherst College in 1826, received the title of M. D. from University of Pennsylvania in Philadelphia 1831, was commissioned missionary physician by the A. B. C. F. M., married Mary A. Tenney of Boston, and sailed for the Sandwich Islands with eighteen others in the whale ship Averick same year, returned after five years' absence on account of the ill health of his wife, and now resides in Winchester, Mass., practicing his profession.

Lucina, born in 1806, remains single and resides in Rochester, N. Y.

Louis, born in 1809, resides in Rochester, N. Y., deals in flour and grain, is a Presbyterian elder, and has held various offices in the city government, and is a corporate member of the A. B. C. F. M.

GENEALOGY OF THE COOLEY FAMILY.

The Cooleys of West Springfield descended from Benjamin Cooley, who came to Springfield in 1640, settled in "the precinct of the Long Meadow," and had a family of ten children; the first being born July 16, 1643. His immediate posterity had large families. His grandson, Obadiah, Jr., and great grandson, Roger, settled in West Springfield.

Obadiah, Jr., made a purchase of land in 1730, "on the west side of the Great River," in Springfield, and in 1738, purchased of Benjamin Ball three acres of land on the bank of the river, now known as the Isaac Humiston place, where he is supposed to have died.

In 1748, his son, Abel, purchased of Moses Miller six acres of land on the corner, opposite his father's homestead, and which, with the exception of the house lot of the late Justin Ely, sold off many years ago, still remains in the possession of his descendants. He was known as Captain Cooley, and had two sons, John and Walter.

John settled in Tatham, on the farm opposite that of Talcott A. Rogers. He had two sons, John, Jr., who died unmarried; and Abel, who left nine children, one of whom, Maria, the widow of James Wallace, resides in her native town, and one, Rev. Henry Cooley, residing in Springfield, are his only survivors.

Walter remained on the ancestral estate, and, surviving his father, died, leaving two sons, Abel and Walter ; the former dying without issue, and the latter leaving two sons and one daughter, Sarah, who, with her mother and brother Richard, now occupies the messuage.

Roger, the great grandson of the patriarch Benjamin, before mentioned, removed from "the precinct of Longmeadow," to West Springfield, in 1759, and settled in "Pauquetuck," having bought a part of the Benjamin Smith estate, and resided thereon until his death, in 1802, at the age of 83. He served as Lieutenant in Col. John Moseley's regiment, stationed at White Plains, in the war of the Revolution, in 1776.

Roger, Jr., the sixth of his ten children, remained with his father on the estate, while his brothers went off for themselves, and he became the possessor of the property. He also served his country in the Revolutionary war, being then very young, and was on duty at the execution of Major Andre. After the war, he became a noted military man, serving several years as Colonel in the Massachusetts militia, and was an honored and worthy officer. He was twice married; his second wife, Electa Smith, surviving him seventeen years, he having died in 1843, at the age of 83 years. He had eight children; the youngest two, Ralph and Mary, being the only representatives in West Springfield of that branch of the Cooley family.

GENEALOGY OF THE DAY FAMILY.

The Day family, in West Springfield, are descended from ROBERT DAY, one of the first settlers of Hartford, Conn., who died in that city in 1648, aged 44. He left two sons, Thomas and John. The descendants of the latter are found in Hartford and Colchester, Conn., Northampton, South Hadley and Monson, Mass., Catskill and various towns in New York and Vermont.

The widow of Robert Day married, for her third husband, Elizur Holyoke, of Springfield, in 1658, and with this may have been connected the removal of her elder son, Thomas, to the town, where he married, the next year, Sarah, daughter of Lieutenant Thomas Cooper, and died December 27, 1711, leaving five sons, Thomas, Samuel, John, Ebenezer and Jonathan. Of these, Thomas, the oldest, removed to Colchester, Conn., and was the ancestor of Rev. Jeremiah Day, D. D.,

LL.D., late President of Yale College, Hon. Thomas Day, LL.D., for many years Secretary of the State of Connecticut, and Rev. Henry N. Day, D. D., of New Haven, Conn., late professor in Western Reserve College.

The next three sons of the first Thomas, viz., Samuel, John and Eleazer, removed to West Springfield, and from them, all of the name in this town are descended, except the family of Pliny Day, who was descended from John, and died in 1846.

Among the descendants of Samuel, the second son of Thomas, who died in 1729, were his son Dea. Samuel Day, of this town, who died in 1773, Mr. Aaron Day, of New Haven, who graduated from Yale College in 1738, and was steward of that institution from 1739 to 1747, the late Mr. Aaron Day of this town, Rev. George E. Day, D. D., professor in the Divinity School of Yale College, Mr. Horace Day, secretary of the Board of Education, in New Haven, Conn., and Hon. Calvin Day, of Hartford, Conn.

From John Day, the third son of Thomas, who died in 1742, the families of the name in Ireland Parish are descended; also the late Heman and Hosea Day, of this town, Hon. Rowland Day, of Moravia, N. Y., who was a member of Congress from the State of New York in 1822 and again in 1832, Mr. Benjamin Day, of Springfield, lately deceased, and Hon. Charles D. Day, of Montreal, Canada, one of the judges of the Court of the Queen's Bench.

From Ebenezer, the fourth son of Thomas, is descended Mr. Julius Day, of this town, whoso sons Austin, Henry and Edmund are residents of Seymour, Ct.

Jonathan, the fifth son of Thomas, lived on the homestead in Springfield, in which place many of his descendants have resided.

In the " Genealogical Register " of the descendants of Robert Day, published in 1848 by Prof. George E. Day, of Yale College, and containing the names of nearly 2500 of the descendants of the first settler, with dates of births, marriages and deaths, it is estimated that the whole number in the direct line, up to that time, was not less than three thousand, and that the same rate of increase for another hundred years, would give from thirty to fifty thousand souls. Twenty-three of the name had, at that time, received a college education, nineteen at Yale, one at Dartmouth, Williams, Amherst and Brown, respectively. Eleven had been, or were then, ministers of the Gospel, generally in the Congregational denomination. The oldest person of the name was Col. Benjamin Day, of this town, who died in the year 1808, in his ninety-eighth year. The average age of those who have become heads of families has been sixty-eight years.

GENEALOGY OF THE ELY FAMILY.

The first of the name, who came to this country, was Nathaniel Ely, who landed at Plymouth, December 25, 1626. He came to Hartford in 1636, to Springfield in 1660, and died here December 25, 1675. He left one son, Samuel.

Samuel Ely had six children, as follows: Samuel, Joseph, Jonathan, John, Mary married Mr. Colman, of Hatfield; Ruth, married Mr. Warner, of Hadley.

John Ely, the fourth son of Samuel, was born at Springfield in 1678, and died in 1758, aged 80 years. He married Mary Bliss, daughter of Samuel Bliss, and had issue as follows: John, Reuben. Abner, Caleb, Noah, Mary, married Luke Bliss; Rachel, married Rev. Jonathan Hubbard.

John Ely, the second, was born 1707, died 1754 Married 1733, to Eunice Colton, and had issue : John, Justin, Eunice, married Roger Newbury; Heman, Rhoda, Amelia, married J. West.

Justin Ely, the second son of John, was born 1739, married Ruth White, 1762, died June 26, 1817, and had issue: Theodore, Anna, Justin, Heman. After the death of Ruth White, 1809, Justin Ely married Mary A. Lane.

Theodore Ely, eldest son of Justin, was born 1764, died 1837. Married Hannah Chandler 1818, and had issue: Hannah, born 1819, married Wm. Kent, of Brooklyn, N. Y.

Justin Ely, second son of Justin, was born 1772, died 1850. Married Lucy Barron 1803, and had issue: Theodore William, died in 1826; Charles, Lucy. Lucy Barron died 1808, and Justin Ely married Abigail Belden 1809, and had issue: Justin, Elizabeth, died October 5, 1837.

Heman Ely, youngest son of Justin the first, was born 1775, married, 1818, Celia Belden, and moved to Elyria, Ohio, where he died, and where his descendants still reside.

Charles Ely, second son of Justin, 2d, was born 1805, married Harriet Kent, and had issue: Louise, Leicester, Harriet. After the death of Harriet Kent, Charles Ely married Eliza Upham, and had issue : Eliza, Charles.

Lucy Barron Ely, daughter of Justin, the 2d, married Dr. Chauncey Belden, and had issue : Theodore, Elizabeth, married Dr. Stephen Bowles ; Herbert.

Justin Ely, youngest son of Justin the 2d, was born 1813, married Nancy H. Lathrop 1854. She died in 1866, and he married Abby French in 1870, and resides in Chicago, Ill.

Homer, Fredric and Cotton Ely, (sons of Cotton, the son of Nathaniel, 3d,) located in Ashleyville, on or near the paternal homestead, married three sisters, daughters of Lieut. Ruggles Kent, reared families, and were valued members of society. Homer and Cotton have recently died, the latter since the Centennial celebration.

James P. Ely, who married Mercy Smith, is the son of Nathan, born 1779; the son of Nathan, born 1759; the son of Samuel, born about 1730; the son of Samuel, born about 1680; the son of Samuel, the only son of Nathaniel the first settler.

Joel Ely, the son of Samuel, married Thankful Leonard, and lived on the common, the spot now occupied by Mrs. Sarah Foster. Their children were, Richard who died in early manhood; Sibyl wife of Dan. Taylor who removed to Turin, N. Y., in 1802 ; Joel ; Abishai ; Thankful, wife of Silas Bannister ; Abigail, wife of John Wood; Ruhaima, wife of Daniel Wood. These last three removed to Windsor, Vt., about 1800.

GENEALOGY OF THE LATHROP FAMILY.

Dr. Joseph Lathrop, the eminent pastor of the West Springfield church, was the only son of Solomon, the son of Joseph, the son of Samuel, the son of Rev. John Lathrop, second pastor of an independent Congregational church in London, England. The first Joseph came to this country and settled in Scituate, Mass., in 1634, afterward in Barnstable, where he died in 1653.

Solomon, son of the second Joseph, born 1706, married Martha Perkins, (Todd,) 1729, died 1733. Their children were Martha, who died young, and Joseph.

Joseph, born 1731, married Elizabeth Dwight, of Hatfield, 1759, ordained in West

Springfield August 25, 1756, died December 31, 1820, in the 90th year of his age, and sixty-fifth of his ministry. His children were, Solomon, born 1760, died 1787; Seth, born 1762, died 1831; Joseph, born 1765, died 1831; Samuel, born 1772, died 1846; Dwight, born 1780, died 1818.

Seth second son of Rev. Dr. Joseph, married Anne Abbott, of Windsor, Ct., 1787, and had issue: Betsey, born 1788, married Rev. Elisha Andrews; Solomon, born 1790, died 1862; Edward, born 1792, died 1863.

Joseph, third son of Rev. Dr. Joseph, married Rowena Wells, of Ellington, Ct., 1790, settled in Wilbraham, and had issue: Joseph, born 1791, died 1833; Wells, born 1795, died 1871; Paoli, born 1797, died 1872; Seth, born 1799, died 1834; Rowena, born 1803, died 1853; Ralph, born 1807, died 1838.

Samuel, fourth son of Rev. Dr. Joseph, married Mary McCrackan, of New Haven, Ct., 1797, and had issue: Nancy H., born 1800, died 1866, married Justin Ely; Samuel, born 1801, died 1825; Mary, born 1802, died 1837, second wife of Rev. Dr. Sprague; William M., born 1806, resides in Newton Mass., John, born 1809; Sarah M., born 1811; Elizabeth D., born 1813, died 1874, married H. Romeyn Vermilye; Joseph, born 1815, resides in St. Louis, Mo.; Henrietta B., born 1817, third wife of Rev. Dr. Sprague; Martha P., born 1819, married Rev Dr. Wood.

Dwight, fifth son of Rev. Dr. Joseph, married Lora Stebbins in 1806, and had issue. Frances, born 1806; Dwight, born 1808; Henry, born 1811; Jere, born 1816.

GENEALOGY OF THE PARSONS FAMILY.

Joseph and Benjamin Parsons were early in the Springfield settlement. Joseph removed to Northampton in 1655. The court records of that town show, that at a court holden in March, 1662, he testified that he was a witness to a deed of the *lands at Springfield*, and a bargain between the Indians and Mr. William Pynchon, dated July 15th, 1636, "for 18 fathoms of wampom, 18 coates, 18 hatchets, 18 hoes and 18 knives." This included all the land now known as Springfield, West Springfield, Agawam, Holyoke, Chicopee, Wilbraham and Longmeadow.

Benjamin Parsons remained at Springfield, was a deacon of the church, and chief actor in its formation. He died August 24, 1689, leaving nine children.

Ebenezer Parsons, son of Benjamin, was a prominent man in West Springfield, and for fifty-two years a deacon of the church. He died September 23, 1752, aged 84. He had nine children. His tombstone still stands in the "old burying ground."

Jonathan Parsons, grandson of Ebenezer, married Mary, daughter of Dea. Joseph Merrick, of West Springfield. He died May 2, 1810, aged 75, and owned the property on the south side of the Park. The house was taken down in 1872.

Jonathan Parsons, son of Jonathan and Mary, purchased his father's estate, married Graty, daughter of Elias Leonard, of Feeding Hills, was an active man in public affairs, an extensive farmer and dealer in farm stock. He died December 6, 1827, and had twelve children.

Edward Parsons, son of Jonathan and Graty, still occupies the homestead that has been in his family for about one hundred and fifty years. He has represented the town and county in the State Senate and House of Representatives. The town is indebted to him for suggesting, arranging and completing the Park, in front of the Town Hall, that previous to 1866, had been an open common.

GENEALOGY OF THE ROGERS FAMILY.

Henry Rogers, born 1733, who was killed by the overturning of a load of wood in 1795, and is buried in the town-house cemetery, lived on the bank of Connecticut river just south of the house now owned by William Fox. His children were Caroline, who married Solomon Ashley and died in 1864; Mahla, who married Hosea Bliss and died 1821; and Asa, who died 1838. Asa had nine children, one of whom, Theodore B., lives in Wethersfield, Ct., and is a representative man; a wagon-maker by trade, and inventor by nature, and the builder of the first railroad car in North Carolina.

Abner, the famous drummer and village blacksmith, who removed to Black River, N. Y., was another branch of the Rogers family. Talcott A., the son of Ely, a thrifty farmer, is still another branch, and the only known resident of that name in town.

GENEALOGY OF THE SMITH FAMILY.

Among the Smiths who came to New England, was a family of four brothers and one sister, as early as 1630, ten years after the landing of the Pilgrims. Mary Smith, the sister, married William Partridge of Hartford, but removed to Hadley, where she remained through life. Christopher lived in Northampton and died childless. Simon seems not to have left any trace of his whereabouts, and his place of abode is not now known. Joseph settled in Hartford and had a family of fifteen children, whose descendants cannot be missed at the present day in that vicinity. The fourth brother, William, was married at Hartford in August, 1644, to Elizabeth Standley, and after residing in Wethersfield and Middletown, settled in Farmington Ct., where he died in January, 1670, leaving nine children.

His sixth child, Benjamin, was born in Farmington in 1658, and after his marriage with Ruth Loomis of Westfield, he removed to that "precinct" and established himself as a resident there, having his homestead near that of Joseph Moseley. But on the 7th of September 1688, when he was thirty years of age, he purchased of John Pynchon of Springfield, several tracts of land in West Springfield, at a place called by the Indians "Pauquetuck," where he commenced the cultivation of the rich intervale land there bordering on the Westfield river, but fearing the consequences of this interference with the aboriginals in the priority of occupation, he wisely, continued his home in Westfield for a year or two, cultivating his land during the summer season, and returning to Westfield every night. But after a sufficient trial of the good faith of the red-skins, he at length ventured to construct a rude kind of house or fort on the plateau at the foot of the mountain slope, which he fortified and guarded against their suspected treachery. Here he made his castle a house of entertainment and protection for the wayward traveler who might be overtaken by nightfall during his meanderings through this primeval forest, for the country had no highways nor roads, except the zigzag cart-path between the trees that led to the Massachusetts Bay, and known as the "Bay path."

Having outlived the feared hostility of the Indians, he was joined by other people, and to facilitate their settlement there, he constructed a saw-mill on the falls of

"Pauquetuck" brook, the foundation timbers of his dam being still embedded in the stream, and when the mill went to decay his mill-saw was preserved and is now in the possession of his great-great-great-grandson in the city of Springfield, and is a specimen of the rude implements in use seventy years after the landing of the Pilgrims on Plymouth Rock, that period having elapsed at the time of building his mill.

He became a great land-holder, and after his death, which occurred in 1738 at the age of 80 years, his estate was distributed, according to his will, by commissioners appointed by the Judge of Probate at Northampton.

The names of Benjamin Smith's children were William; Ruth, who married Samuel Taylor; Samuel; Elizabeth, who married Ebenezer Miller, Jr.; Rachael, who married Samuel Morgan; Jonathan; Job; and Mary, who married Ebenezer Day.

Jonathan and Job were executors of their father's will, and remained on the estate, the latter occupying his father's dwelling, while Benjamin lived in a house built for him a little west of his father's house.

Jonathan had a large and stately house erected for his use just east of the brook, on a commanding eminence at the junction of two roads, having married Margaret, the only child of Samuel Ball of West Springfield Center. The names of his seven children were Jonathan; David; Solomon; Caleb; Daniel; Margaret, who married Stephen Miller; and Simeon.

Mr. Ball having died, his second wife surviving him, it was found by his will, that he had devised his real estate, with the exception of his homestead, to the children of his daughter, and the child of his second wife by a former marriage, so that the "great swamp," as it was called, now known as Ball's swamp, with other large tracts of land, fell into the possession of the Smith family, and Jonathan, Jr. and David, the two older sons, took up their abode with their step-grandmother, and assisted in the cultivation of the farm, where Jonathan remained during his life; but David, after the death of his father, sold out there, and removed to Pauquetuck, and occupied jointly with his brother Solomon, the house and lands situated northerly of their father's residence, subsequently purchasing his brother's interest in the same. Solomon resided in the neighborhood until his death; Caleb removed to Vermont; Daniel remained on his father's homestead; and Simeon, removing to New Lebanon Springs, returned after the death of his wife, and remained on the old homestead with his brother, until death. Jonathan had seven children, David had six, Solomon four, Caleb three, Daniel five, and Simeon one.

Of the descendants of Benjamin Smith, only seven households bearing the name of Smith are remaining in West Springfield. There are residing in Springfield, three, and one in Troy, N. Y. There are others whose residences in the West are not now known to the writer. One Smith family removed to Chester, one to Mendon, one to Warehouse Point, Conn., and several more to the States of New York and Vermont. Of the large estate of the first settler, all has been transferred to parties of other names, except a tract occupied by John D. Smith, in the south-west corner of the town, which has not been allowed to pass out of the Smith family. On this tract stands a stately and venerable white oak tree; majestic in appearance, and known to be more than a century old, yet showing no signs of decay. Part of Gen. Burgoyne's army passed under it in their march from their defeat at Saratoga to Massachusetts.

The Smiths have never exhibited any propensity for contributing to the ministerial ranks, but many of them have been teachers of the public schools, some physicians, one a high sheriff, several artisans, and some statesmen, one having served his constituency several years in the Legislature, dying at Boston while in service.

Solomon served in the war with the French. David served in the Revolutionary war, his son David serving as musician in the same regiment with his father, in the company of Capt. Levi Ely, of West Springfield, who was killed in an encounter with the tories and Indians lying in ambush.

Simeon Smith was a scientist in his day, and during the Revolutionary war manufactured saltpetre at Pauquetuck for government use. He also distilled New England rum for the army, using for that purpose the expressed juice of our common maize, after fermentation. His machinery is in existence to this day, at Pauquetuck.

David, Solomon and Daniel Smith, in the winter of 1766, contracted with the building committee to furnish two hundred bushels of lime, for the construction of a "brick meeting-house," in the "precinct of Longmeadow," and promptly manufactured the commodity ready for the builders. But one of the building committee becoming "miffed" at the conduct of the others, broke down the project of building, so the lime was neither used nor paid for, resulting in a total loss to the manufacturers.

Jonathan Smith, the seventh child of Benjamin, was born in 1697, and seems to have been the prince of Pauquetuck, being the business man of the neighborhood, and friendly adviser for all. He was a very conscientious man, and strict as a Jewish patriarch. No unnecessary work was allowed to be performed on his premises after the going down of the sun on Saturday, until the close of the Sabbath; and on one occasion, his son David, when a grown-up man, returned home from a hunting excursion, for which he was said to be famous, after sundown on Saturday; his father obliged him, with unshaven face, to go four miles to the old church on the common, the next day, so scrupulous was he in his observance of the Lord's day.

The ancient headstone at his grave, in "Paucatuck Cemetery," thus announces his fame:

"In memory of Mr. Jona. Smith, (The virtuous Father of a numerous offspring, to whom he gave an Example of Piety and Prudence,) who died February 9, A. D. 1772, in the 75th year of his age."

Simeon Smith came here from South Hadley, when a boy of 16 years, to learn the trade of joiner and cabinet-maker of Nathaniel Gaylord, in Tatham. During his apprenticeship, the Revolutionary war broke out, and he went into service in the army. After his return, he continued here until his death, which occurred in 1843, at the age of 90 years. His residence was in Shad Lane, where he reared a family of ten children, only two of whom are still living. It is not known that he was related to the descendants of Benjamin Smith, of Pauquetuck.

GENEALOGY OF THE STEBBINS FAMILY.

Benjamin Stebbins, who settled in West Springfield, was the son of Joseph, the son of Thomas, the son of Rowland, who was born in Suffolk County, England, 1594, sailed from Ipswich in ship Francis 1634, first settled in Roxbury, removed to Springfield 1639, and died at Northampton 1671.

Benjamin, the son of Joseph, born 1677, died 1748, married Martha Ball, and had issue: Benjamin, Francis, Martha, Miriam, Mary, Mercy.

Benjamin, 2d, born 1702, died 1783, married Mary Day, and had issue: Benjamin and Vashti.

Benjamin, 3d, born 1727, died 1803, married Sabra Lyman, and had issue: Benjamin, Francis, Jere, Sabra, Solomon, Edward, Lovicy, Clement, Festus; these last died in infancy.

Jere and Solomon settled in West Springfield.

Jere Stebbins, born 1757, died 1817, married Elizabeth Brewster, and had issue: Betsey, born 1779, died 1834, married Jabez D. De Witt, of Montreal, P. Q.; Lora, born 1782, died 1860, married Dwight Lathrop; Polly, died in infancy; Pama, born 1786, died 1866, married Reuben Champion; Benjamin, born 1788, died 1819, married Maritta Parsons; Miner, born 1791, died 1828; Polly, Francis and Maria, all died young.

Solomon, son of Benjamin 3d, born 1763, died 1813, married Mahala Day, and had issue: Sally, born 1789, died 1853; Charles, born 1788, died 1864; Heman, born 1791, died 1838, and was a lawyer in Brookfield; Sabra, born 1793, died 1867, married Harry Palmer.

GENEALOGY OF THE WADE FAMILY.

James Wade, a native of Medford, Mass., born July, 1750, died May, 1826, married Mary, daughter of Rev. Edward Upham, January 15, 1780. Their children, all born in Feeding Hills, Mass., were Martha, born 1782, died 1863, 81 years; Nancy, born 1786, died 1865, 79; Mary, born 1787, died 1866, 79; James, born 1789, died 1868, 79; Sidney, born 1793, died 1847, 54; Theodore, born 1797, died 1863, 70; Charles, born 1798; Benjamin F., born 1800; Edward, born 1802, died 1866, 64.

James, the father, was a shoe-maker and common soldier, was at the battles of Lexington and Bunker Hill, and was confined for a long time a prisoner at Halifax. He removed to Andover, O., in 1821, traveling, as was the custom of those times, with an ox team and covered wagon. Benjamin F. and Edward claim to have walked the entire distance. The sons were self-educated, and for a time all school-teachers.

James settled in Watervliet, N. Y., was a physician and had an extensive practice.

Theodore, Charles and Sydney became farmers and settled in Andover, O.

Edward studied law and settled in Cleveland, O. He was a great temperance and abolition advocate, a member of Congress, and committee on commerce from 1853 to 1861. He is said to have been one of the ablest lawyers of the Cleveland bar, honest, high-minded, a genuine democrat.

Benjamin Franklin Wade, distinguished as a zealous opponent of slavery, resides in Ashtabula county, Ohio. He taught school and studied law in his youth; was admitted to the bar in 1828; was elected a member of the Ohio Senate in 1837; was chosen presiding judge of the third judicial district in that State, in 1847; was sent to the U. S. Senate in 1851; was re-elected Senator for six years, in 1857; was made President of the Senate in 1867; having been selected for that office on account of his resolute character, and inflexible fidelity to the cause of liberty, and has been honored with many trusts. In the early days of the Rebellion, he was appointed chairman of the joint committee on the conduct of the war. In 1871 he was one of the commission to visit San Domingo, and report on its annexation to the United States, and is now attorney for the Northern Pacific Railroad.

GENEALOGY OF THE WHITE FAMILY.

Elder John, who came from England to Cambridge, Mass., in 1632, is the father of most of this name in New England. Daniel, the son of Deacon Nathaniel, the son of Captain Nathaniel, the son of Elder John, came from Hadley and settled in West Springfield about 1715. His son Daniel, was a carpenter, and built a house of hewn logs, on the north side of Meeting-house hill, which stood till about 1850. Here were born to him Horace, the father of Sewall, the father of Homer and William; Pliny, the father of Daniel G. and Daniel G., Jr., and Edward, the father of Edward, the father of Chauncey. The last named of each of these branches now own, in part, the homesteads of their grandfathers.

Henry White, connected with the Heman Day family, is the son of Julius, the son of Elijah, the son of Joel, the son of Captain Daniel, the son of Lieutenant Daniel, the son of Elder John.

Francis and Joseph White, are sons of Jared, the son of Martin, the son of Preserved, the son of Preserved, the son of Daniel, who first settled in West Springfield.

GENEALOGY OF THE BLISS FAMILY.

Thomas Bliss, an early settler of Hartford, Ct., died there in 1640. His widow, Margaret, removed to Springfield in 1646, with four sons and four daughters; leaving Thomas, her eldest son, married at Saybrook, whence he removed to Norwich.

Of the four sons who came to Springfield, Mass., with their mother, the second was Lawrence. He died 1676.

Lawrence married Lydia Wright, October 25, 1654. They had nine children. Of these, the youngest, Pelatiah, was born August 19, 1674. He died January 2, 1747-8.

Pelatiah married Elizabeth Hitchcock, April 21, 1698. They had nine children. Caleb, the eighth, married Editha Day, January 5, 1739-40. Deacon Caleb, (the father,) died May 22, 1758.

Deacon Caleb and Editha had eight children. Pelatiah, ("Colonel Pelatiah,") was the fifth. He married Ruth Woodworth in 1773; died October 29, 1828.

Col. Pelatiah had six children. Jeduthan, the eldest, was born April 10, 1774; married Susannah Tracey, 1805. They had eight children, of whom Luke, the present post-master of Mittineaque, is one, and Susan, wife of John D. Smith, of Tatham, another.

Miss Sophia, a daughter of Col. Pelatiah, born March 19, 1781, still resides with her niece, Mrs. Ruth Beals, in Sunderland, Mass.

The youngest son of Widow Margaret Bliss, was John. He married Patience Burt, 1667, and died September 20, 1702. John and Patience had seven children. Ebenezer, the seventh, was born 1683; married Joanna Lamb; had eight children, and died November 4, 1761. Rev. John was the seventh of these; born June 6, 1736; ordained November 9, 1765; married ——— White, of Bolton, Ct., and had six children, as follows: John, Betsey, Achsah, Joel W., Hosea and Daniel. Achsah married Ruggles Kent, who came from Suffield, Ct., and settled in West Springfield. Hosea, "Uncle Hosea" as he was commonly called, married ———Rogers, and was the chief blacksmith of Ashleyville, for many years. William Bliss, one of the sons of Hosea, still resides in Ashleyville.

REMINISCENCES OF WEST SPRINGFIELD.

In the early days, one Cooper, a farm laborer, agreed with one Ashley, a farmer, to work six months, at $7 per month; but if for a longer time, he would work at a less rate. Farmer Ashley finally bargained for seven months at $6 per month, which was perfectly satisfactory.

The standard price of land in Chicopee field was, for some time, twenty shillings per acre; but one tract of seven acres, belonging to a man by the name of Bagg, was actually sold for a "Barlow" knife (a choice specimen of English pocket cutlery).

SEYMOUR BAGG.

About the year 1800, Mr. Jonathan Brooks dug potatoes in Chicopee field, and took them on an ox cart to "Skipmug," now Chicopee Falls, and sold them for a shilling a bushel. There was neither bridge nor ferry at Chicopee then, and he drove by the way of Springfield bridge, a distance of about ten miles both ways fording the Chicopee river, in order to reach the Ames paper mill employes.

REUBEN BROOKS.

Dr. Lathrop was a short, broad-shouldered man, and, in his latter days, had a tremulous motion and a gruff voice. For nearly twenty years, he visited his brother minister, the Rev. Bezaleel Howard, of the First Church in Springfield, twice a week, usually riding horseback, as he was fond of this exercise. CHARLES HOWARD.

Dr. Lathrop once was somewhat annoyed in trying to bore a hole through a short stick for a beetle, when a half-witted fellow suggested his putting it in a hog's trough, to keep it from turning; which idea was used and pleased the doctor greatly.

Dr. Lathrop composed with rapidity, and wrote with a quill, turning it round and round, one quill lasting to write several sermons. He usually made his pastoral visits on Monday and Tuesday. He lived with great economy, and no carpet was in his house for many years. He always dressed in black, and when his coat faded, a tailoress came to the house and turned it. Madame Lathrop, also, dressed in plain homespun, and, although she lived in the days of hoop skirts and corsets, she never considered them a necessary appendage to the dress of a minister's wife * She superintended well her household, and on every day in the year, except Sunday, a boiled Indian pudding was served at her dinner-table. SEWALL WHITE.

---

* There are, in the Springfield Museum, specimens of the corsets and hoops used in West Springfield, previous to the year 1800.

At Dr. Sprague's ordination, in 1819, the event was so unusual there was a great gathering, and when the church doors were opened, the press was so great that coats were torn, and boys trampled on. Stands, for the sale of gingerbread and watermelons, were erected on the north side of the church. AARON BAGG.

The large trees that adorn Ramapogue street, were set by Lewis and Ebenezer Day and John Ely, about the year 1774, and were dug at Barber's swamp, back of the house of Hiram Carter, in Tatham. Mr. Lewis Day, who lived to be eighty, and died in Deerfield, N. Y., inquired of Mr. Julius Day, who was visiting him in his last years, if those trees were standing and appreciated. When assured they were, he replied, "Then I get pay for setting them." Ebenezer Day lived near the house now occupied by Samuel Smith. The house had diamond-shaped window-panes, and was pulled down about 1830.

JULIUS DAY.

The large button-woods, near the house of Joseph Morgan, in Chicopee, were set by Darius Ely, when a hired man for Abner Morgan, in 1782. SAMUEL MORGAN.

June 25, 1776, when a draft was made for the army, forty-four men were assigned Springfield, and forty-eight West Springfield.

1775. West Springfield sent fifty-three men to the war, under command of Capt. Enoch Chapin and Lieutenants Samuel Flower and Luke Day.

News of the battle of Lexington reached Springfield at noon on the second day after it occurred, and the next morning, Col. Patterson's regiment started thence for Boston.

The Shay's Rebellion, squelched January 24, 1787, was aided by the brave Capt. Luke Day, who, after seven years' honorable service in the Revolutionary war, fell into its advocacy at the old Stebbins tavern, now occupied as a private residence by Mr. Lucien Bliss. Adjutant Elijah Day, Benjamin Ely and Daniel Luddington were his associates and abettors. Capt. Day drilled his men on the common, armed them with hickory clubs, and uniformed them with hemlock sprigs. Once they seized the Springfield ferry and searched every man who passed. The government party were distinguished by slips of white paper on their hats.

A newspaper, called the "American Intelligencer," was established in West Springfield, August, 1795. Richard Davidson, an Englishman, was the proprietor. Edward Gray soon after bought it, and continued it, weekly, for three years, doing, also, job work, when he removed to Suffield, Conn., and still later, to Hartford. Mr. Gray's office was a few rods west of the old meeting-house.

The Hampden Grays were a famous military company, organized in West Springfield, in 1832, and noted throughout the State for accuracy, promptitude, and the neatness of their uniforms and drill. Linus Bagg, Edward Parsons, Henry Parsons and Enoch N. Smith, were successively its captains, and every private seemed to take pride in its exploits. By a change of law, it was disbanded about 1840.

Nathan Ely, born 1759, was an officer's waiter at the age of 17, in the Revolutionary war. While at Albany, N. Y., the officer had a consultation about sending a reliable man to Boston for supplies. From an adjoining room, young Ely overheard the remark, "Send Ely, he is an honest devil, and never swears."

Dr. Lathrop's prestige in divinity did not destroy his sociability with the common people He employed farm help, and was jovial with them. At sheep-shearing time, it was his custom to go and visit the shearers every forenoon, and enliven their monotonous employment by the relation of circumstances and events of the past. His men always knew when he was about to leave them, because he was in the habit of reserving the most unreliable and unlikely story for the last, and when that came on the docket and was under way, his departure was inevitable.

Thompson Phillips lived at "Aries Little," opposite Mittineaque, and was the leading joker of the town. On town meeting days he stood the "head centre" of attraction for the assembled multitude. Some of his jokes were very personal and pointed. At one time, he gathered a quantity of sorrell seed, and peddled it around as grass seed, under the representation of a new variety, called "Flare Top." At another time, he procured some pamphlets, made entirely of plain white paper, without any writing or printing on them, and offered them for sale as the "*dying man's speech*," many persons taking them at his word without examination; but, when confronted by his victims, he got off by exclaiming: "Oh; he died without saying anything." His like does not reside hereabouts now. His propensity for curt joking was not diminished by the approach of death; for, in one instance when a neighbor was dangerously sick, he cautiously opened the back door of the sick man's house, and inquired in respectful tone after the condition of the sick man, and on being informed that no change was apparent, he gravely inquired, "Are there any hopes of his death, marm?" And many like deeds did this man do.

Jerre Stebbins kept a small store of goods, and exchanged them with the farmers for their productions. Among his commodities for sale were some small grindstones, leaning against the outside of the store One day, Phillips got a farmer to enter the store and inquire of Mr. Stebbins how much he paid for cheese; the price was named, and the farmer promised to bring one in. Phillips and his comrades, in the meantime, had papered up a small grindstone, outside the store, and the farmer delivered it upon the counter, while Phillips and his comrades stood watching for the explosion of the merchant as he opened the package.

PUBLIC LIBRARIES.

A library with forty subscribers, headed by Rev. Dr. Lathrop, was started December, 1775, and divided among the shareholders, October, 1807. It attained the magnitude of fifty-six volumes, was kept in a two-bushel basket, and made the circuit of the parish, lodging with the most responsible families.

Another library started in 1810, which never exceeded the capacity of an ordinary cupboard, had its head-quarters at the Town House, and was divided by sale about the year 1840. The present Town library, founded by individual subscriptions about 1854, is increasing in patronage, and has already attained about 1,500 volumes.

THE OLD SCHOOL-HOUSE ON THE COMMON.

This structure, as near as can be ascertained, was erected in the year 1740, and stood upon the Common, east of the old Meeting-house, among a group of scattered trees, which lent a *shade* of pleasantness to the locality. The style of its architecture is nameless, but has been in use for centuries, and was the base from which has been developed the details of the French style of house building, by Mansard and others, but was known here as the gambrel roof pattern. The frame is still sound and firm, and must have been carefully put together, the size being forty feet long, twenty feet wide and twelve feet high from sill to eaves. It was finished with only one outside door, placed in the middle of the front or south side, two windows each side of the door, two in each end, and four in the back side of the house. It was covered with narrow clapboards, exposing between three and four inches in width to the weather, which appear to have once been painted white. A chimney was placed in each end of the house, each containing two fireplaces big enough to contain "back-log and fore-stick," according to the usage of the times.

The lower story was divided into an east and west room, by a hall four feet wide, leading from the front door to the rear of the building, and were used by the smaller scholars, and in which Ann Cooley taught the children for twenty successive years.

The upper room, which occupied the entire length and width of the building, was in the "*French roof*," and was reached by a flight of stairs starting at the back end of the hall, and turning to the west by one

THE BIG ELM.

broad stair. It was lighted by two windows in each end, three dormer windows in the front, and two in the rear, and warmed in winter by two blazing fires in the fire-places at each end of the room. In this room was kept the "*High School*" of the town, inasmuch as it was the only one kept in the second story, and served as a college for the large boys and girls, in which, for the period of eighty years, the free dispensation of knowledge and birch, has been made according to law, and it is difficult for the human mind to comprehend the full complement of the two commodities named, that have been wielded during the four-score years of their application. How many an unlucky wight, whose diurnal duties brought him to this place, has had his soul blighted and crushed with the application of the embers-drawn stick, as each successive blow came basting across his back, or his calves made to tingle with the repeated applications of *government*, from the strong hand of the knight, whose duty it was to reign, teach and punish. How many light and tender hearts have been made heavy and sad in the bosoms of the wayward girls, by the withering look, shot like an arrow to the soul, from him who presided over the realm of that long and busy room, the reader can never know, but is left in his reflections to conjecture, that not a few hearts in that sovereign apartment have found their several affinities, and opportunities "to meet and mingle."

For several years before the building went into disuse for the purposes of education, the school district, like all similar organizations, was the scene of annual clamorings by "men of many minds," for a new house, or some improvement of the old, and votes to rebuild or repair, were annually made, and as often rescinded, until the year 1818, when the district voted to raise $800 for a new school-house, which was raised and expended in a brick structure, containing three school-rooms on the first floor, and a hall in the second story for the use of the town, which being completed in 1820, the old school-house on the Common was sold and moved away, after having served the purposes of the education of youth for eighty years. It now stands on the grounds of William White, in use as a storehouse, and is in a good state of preservation after a life of one hundred and thirty-four years.

THE BIG ELM.

One of the largest trees in the State, is the great Elm standing on land of Mrs. Heman Smith, and Mrs. A. W. Allen, situated on the west side of Main street, in West Springfield. The land it occupies was formerly a part of the farm of the late Heman Day, Esq., and the tree was set by him on his twenty-first birthday, January 27, 1776, he having brought it out of the West Springfield meadows on his shoulder, it being then a thrifty tree of eight or ten years' growth. He set other trees in the vicinity, but this was his favorite tree, and his dwelling being on the opposite side of the street, he daily watched its luxuriant growth for sixty-one years, at which period he was gathered to his fathers, at the honored age of eighty-two years.

The tree flourished wonderfully, and drew the admiration of many persons from afar. The cut herein presented, was engraved from a photograph of the tree, taken in 1874, and is a correct representation of its features and dimensions; the circumference of its trunk, at its smallest diameter, measuring on the surface of the outer bark, traverses the space of twenty-seven feet; its branches extend a distance of one hundred and twelve feet, thus sheltering an area of nine thousand, eight hundred and fifty-two square feet, and overhanging a circumference of three hundred and fifty-two lineal feet, affording shade for a regiment of men. The trunk appears to be sound, and the foliages hows a full-sized leaf, as fresh as a tree of twenty years' growth.

It is to be hoped that this last of the big trees of the original "Agawam," will be spared by the woodman's axe, and the day far in the distant future when the revolving cycle of time shall lay low this splendid specimen of vegetable growth, emblem of symmetry and of strength; having already braved the tempests of more than a century, with not a friendly companion standing near to shield it from the blasts of the pitiless storm.

THE OLD MEETING-HOUSE ON THE COMMON.

It is difficult to do justice to the memory of this unique and demolished structure, because of the conflicting opinions in regard to its construction; but its history is not entirely obscure.

In May, 1695, the inhabitants of Springfield living on the west side of the "Great River," consisting of thirty-two families, presented a petition to the "Great and General Courte," that they "might be permitted to invite and settle a minister," and the town of Springfield appointed a committee to follow the petitioners to the "Courte," and object to that permission. But the "Courte" investigated the matter, and in November, 1696, "ordered that said petitioners be permitted, and allowed, to invite, procure, and settle, a learned and orthodox minister, on the west side of Connecticut river, to dispense the word of God unto those that dwell there, and that they be a distinct and separate precinct for that purpose."

In June, 1698, the church was formed, and the Rev. John Woodbridge was constituted its first pastor, but it does not appear that the inhabitants had any particular place for worship during the first four years of their organization as a church. The inhabitants of the "pre-

THE FIRST MEETING-HOUSE.

BUILT IN 1702.

cint," however, commenced the erection of a "meeting-house," and it was completed June 24, 1702, much to their joy and satisfaction. One writer has said that it remained for one hundred and eighteen years, "a curious specimen of ancient architecture, and a monument of the piety and zeal of our fathers;" the architect being John Allys, of Hatfield, who, twenty-five years previously had erected on the east side of the river, the second meeting-house ever built in Springfield, to take the place of the first small structure, the dimensions of which were twenty-five feet wide, by forty feet long, erected in 1645, by John Burr, the first carpenter who ever penetrated the "Bay Path" from the coast to Connecticut river.

The timber for the construction of the meeting-house, was prepared from trees grown on the common, near the spot where the house was placed, and the inhabitants were so few, that all the men and boys of the precinct, could find room to be all seated at once upon the sills of the house after the frame was raised. The house was forty-two feet square, and ninety-two feet in height. The first story, constituting audience room and galleries, was covered with four steep, uniform high roofs, each side being of equal dimensions, and upon each of the four roofs projected a triangular dormer gable, pierced with a window. This story was finished with three outside doors, one each in the center of the south, east and west sides, and two windows each side of the doors with corresponding windows above them to light the galleries. The pulpit, placed on the north side, occupying the place of a doorway, was lighted by one window on each side.

Above this story was placed another much smaller than the first, having one window on each side of the story, and high roofs and gables like the one below. Upon this was erected a third story, smaller than the second, with corresponding roofs and gables, the body portion of the story having on each side a large opening, to serve the purpose of a bell room; thus making a succession of houses, one surmounting the other, each being correspondingly and symmetrically smaller than the one directly beneath it.

The upper superstructure supported a strong iron rod, on which was mounted a huge vane of sheet iron, through which were cut several devices, and also the figures 1702, the date of the erection of the house. Above this was perched an ambitious rooster, the ever-cherished weather-cock of those days, whose reckonings of the weather would beat Sir Robert B. Thomas' Almanac, and even Old Probabilities himself. This animal, and also the one on the meeting-house on the east side of the river, were imported from England; composed of gilded copper, and were each four feet in length. One is still in use on the First Church in Springfield, but the whereabouts of our chanticleer rests in oblivion.

The structure was clapboarded, but was never painted. All the windows were small, made of leaden sash and glazed with small diamond-shaped glass.

The second story was supported by two pairs of massive beams set transversely, and resting on the eaves-plates of the first story, depending on which were the four corner posts of the second story, which ran down several feet below the cross timbers, terminating in the shape of a heart, being interlocked to the cross beams, and ran up to the eaves of the second story; these four cross timbers operating as sills for the second story.

The whole of the interior of the first story, up to the closing of the roof at the commencement of the second story, was all open, exposing to view beams, studding, rafters and outside boarding, with no inside finish above the window stools, a floor being laid at the bottom of the second story, which closed in the audience-room and galleries.

The flooring of the audience-room seems to have been placed independent of the frame-work of the sills of the house, composed of sleepers supported by independent piers, and so low that the floor was down to the bottom of the sills, making it necessary to step over the sill down to the floor—a very awkward method of entering any house; but Westfield had a meeting-house with entrance in like manner, which was a stumbling-block to many. Two flights of stairs led up to the galleries, in the south-easterly and south-westerly corners, commencing each side of the front door, and rising to a broad stair in each, directing the course northerly on each side. Around the walls were fifteen large, square pews, occupying all the space not occupied by the pulpit, door-ways, and stair-ways. In the central part of the house were two rows of long slips, fronting the pulpit, with a partition between them, one division being occupied by the men, and the other by the women. This arrangement would of course make one aisle on the east, and one on the west side of the house. The pulpit, the pews, and the railing were of oak, and yellow pine timber; the pews were finished with open work at the top of the seat back, the top railing being supported by spindle-shaped balusters, and the rails were large and clumsy. Of the size, style and height of the pulpit, nothing definite is now known. It was furnished with a sounding-board over the speaker, which, by reacting the emanating flow of sound from his voice, saved the articulation of his words from becoming lost in the reverberant regions of the cross timbers and braces of the roof above.

In this house our forefathers assembled for worship at the beating of a drum, for the space of forty-one years A bell was then procured, which, after eighteen years' faithful service in the call to prayers, and in the knell of the fallen, its clear ringing tones became hushed by the frost of a crisp cold Sabbath morning in the depth of winter. It was, however, re-cast, and again put upon duty in the old church tower, and at three subsequent periods has been submitted to the crucible for reconstruction from like causes. In 1802, it was transferred from its familiar locality under the vane and weather-cock, to the new church on the hill, where it still continues to sound the call to prayers, and to peal forth the solemn notes of warning to the people, that human life is surely approaching its end. For one hundred and thirty years has this faithful and true sentinel continued on every Lord's day to call the inhabitants together for the worship of God, yet, how many heed not the call. On the other hand, there have been some who have hailed with joy the sound of that friendly call to the house of God, and eternity alone shall reveal the amount of tender emotion and reverential regard it has awakened in the bosoms of His followers as the "sound of the church-going bell" invited them to join in His praise and worship. Its last re-cast was in February, 1825, when additional metal was used to enlarge its size.

The inhabitants of the "precinct" had occupied their meeting-house, oblivious of time, for forty-six years, at which period, Obadiah Frary, of Northampton, constructed a "meeting-house clock," and it was placed within the tower, but the construction of the house was such, that the leaks, in times of driving storms, had so affected the wooden clock as to render it unfit for duty, and it was finally taken away after a service of twenty-five or thirty years.

As time advanced, the meeting-house was becoming more and more dilapidated, and many unsuccessful attempts were made to agree on a spot for a new meeting-house, and after it had been in use eighty-four years, the parish gave liberty to individuals to repair it, and the house was considerably remodeled; the gables were taken away, a ceiling was constructed over the galleries, extending across from one eaves-plate to the other; pews were put in place of the two rows of slips, and wood sash and crown glass, in room of the leaden sash and diamond glass; new flooring was added, placing the floor on a level with the sills; the repairs incurring an expenditure of between five and six hundred dollars. The house was used sixteen years after these repairs, when it was abandoned for the new one on the hill.

The last Sabbath assemblage in this house, was June 20, 1802, when the pastor, Rev. Joseph Lathrop, D. D., preached a valedictory sermon from the ninth verse of the forty-eighth Psalm. In closing, he said: "The antiquity of this house carries our minds back to the time of its erection, one hundred years ago. This community was then small, consisting of but thirty families; savages dwelt among them, and a wilderness surrounded them. There are no houses here except this ancient house of God, which were built a hundred years ago. The founders of this ancient temple are gone, and their places on earth are known no more. The same in a century will be said of us. We are now about to leave this house; this is the last time that we are here to meet for God's worship; there will soon be a last time of our meeting in any place on earth. May we all meet in Heaven." Four days after the delivery of this farewell address, Dr. Lathrop assembled his flock in the new church on the hill, to assist in the dedication of that, "which day completed One Hundred Years from the erection of the First Church."

Thus was this unique house of worship occupied for the long period of one century, by a patient, devoted people, without any plaster or paint on the inside or outside, nor was there ever a fire kindled within its walls; the women being favored with the use of "foot stoves," containing live coals, which by noon had become ashes, and in the intermission were replenished with coals from landlord Stebbins' bar-room fire-place; while the men in winter were supposed to be invincible to that principle, termed the "negative of heat;" and our forefathers often referred in after life to the fact, that they were often required to sit, of a cold Sabbath morning in winter, and give ear to the delivery of a sermon, whose divisions ran as high as *sixteenthly* and *seventeenthly*, when the keenness of the air had absorbed a majority of the heat from their extremities.

The house remained from 1802 to 1820, for the accommodation of funeral occasions, town meetings and other gatherings, when, by a vote of the parish, it was taken down, the building having served its day and generation, for the term of one hundred and eighteen years. Miss Betsy Loveland taught a sewing-school there.

It is related of Mr. Jonathan Parsons, about the time of the Revolutionary war, that while driving a five cattle team, (two yoke of oxen and a horse,) attached to a cart load of stalks, when near the southern entrance of Shad Lane, two horsemen overtook him and ordered him to turn out for the coach of Gen. Washington. Not knowing that Washington was expected, and doubting the couriers' word, he refused, declaring he had as good a right to the road as the General. Soon after a coach passed, having forded the Agawam river, near the house of Mr. James Leonard, on its way to the Springfield ferry. Parsons halted his team near Ferry street, and followed the coach. The boat was on the east side of the river, and while waiting for it, the couriers spoke of the teamster that refused to turn out. Parsons overheard Washington say: "That man was right, he had as good a right to the road as I have."

The following extract is from the Springfield Republican, of March 23, 1872.

"AN OLD LANDMARK GONE."

Mr. J. N. Bagg's large brown house in West Springfield, close on the brink of the road and the bank of the river, directly opposite the "double ditch" shad fishery, was taken down on Saturday. It was an old structure, how old the oldest inhabitant knoweth not, but its age is supposed to be at least 125 years. Native octogenarians say it was an old house when they first knew it. That it belonged to a past age is evidenced by the fact that the original clapboards and lath were both of rived oak, and all put on with wrought hand-made nails. The clapboards were about four and one-half feet long, and evidently shaved on one side. It was a stately structure, and the timbers were all hewn, and of such sterling stuff as white oak and yellow pine. The frame was mortised, dove-tailed and pinned together so firmly that it was a difficult work to throw it down, even after it was stripped for the sacrifice. Some of the principal timbers were eight to twelve inches square, and the joists three by five inches, and planed and beaded on the exposed sides. Eight white-oak posts supported the building, and these are sixteen and one-half feet long, and range from eight inches square at the base, to twelve inches at the shoulder. Some of the floor boards are eighteen inches wide by twenty feet long, and good for another generation. A chimney with five separate flues and three brick ovens occupied fifteen feet square in the center of the house, and the mantle-pieces were of oak, fourteen inches square, and ran the whole length of the chimney. The bricks were of the largest size, and laid in clay. No traces of the exact age of the house have been found, but it is believed to have been built for a boatman's tavern by one of the Stebbins family, an early settler there. Under its floor were found two or three old coins, including a George II. penny, the date of 1749, in an excellent state of preservation.

REV. JUSTIN PERKINS, D. D.,

Was one of the remarkable men of the town. He was born in 1805, in what is known as Rock Valley, in Ireland Parish. He was brought up on a farm, had a studious turn of mind, entered Amherst College at the age of twenty, graduated in 1829, was College tutor one year, studied theology two years at Andover, was ordained a missionary, June, 1833, in the church on Meeting-House hill, and embarked with his wife for Persia, in September of the same year. He spent in all, thirty-six years in the Nestorian field; founded the mission there, had charge of the mission press, and was the author of several books published in that country and America. His great work was the translation of the entire Bible, into the modern Syriac language. His last return to America was in August, 1869, where he died December 31st of the same year, and he is buried near the place of his birth. His only surviving child, Rev. Henry M. Perkins, is the pastor of a Congregational church, in Fremont, Me.

Obituary of Richard Bagg, Jr., (born 1812, died 1852, No. 147, in the

Pedigree on page 112,) abridged from a sketch in the "New England Farmer," 1854.

In boyhood, he was remarkable for an activity and intelligence beyond his years. His promptitude and youthful manliness made him the pride of his parents and the villagers. His was no mediocrity of attainment. He was first and foremost both in the school-room and play-ground; a leader rather than a follower; bold, without being impudent, punctilious, without being mean, and shrewd, without being treacherous. His love of books was extreme, and everything within his reach was read with astonishing avidity. At Monson Academy, he showed great proficiency, and was rapidly fitting himself for college, when ill-health forced him to abandon his books and come home, as his friends thought, to die of consumption.

But he would not be idle, and activity, which had always characterized him, continued to be his ruling passion. The first hot-beds known to the town soon appeared in his father's garden, and other unwonted improvements in farm life, attracted general attention and remark. His health improved, under a rigid system of diet and exercise, and he was entrusted with the sale of the farm produce. The memory of the grand success of his first attempt as a market man, when he sold a load of his father's pumpkins for the magnificent sum of ten dollars, never quite deserted him. As he approached to manhood, several of his winters were devoted to school teaching, both in his native town and at Brimfield, at Monson, and finally, at Jamaica, L. I., where his health again broke down and forced him to devote himself henceforth exclusively to out door life.

In fifteen years from the beginning of his agricultural operations, he became the largest gardener in the county, if not in the State, having about forty acres under cultivation, some of which, produced two and three crops a year. He had several acres each of asparagus and onions, and in the busiest season of the year had been known to employ upwards of sixty persons. He was regular and precise in all his movements, and required regularity and precision in all whom he controlled. Every workman had a specially labelled hook for his hat and clothing, and every tool and implement had its place and was thoroughly cleansed after using. Printed regulations for the government of his workmen, were to be seen about his buildings.

Everything he undertook was vigorously carried to its completion. He considered a matter well before he enlisted in it, but once engaged he entered with all his might. In this was the secret of the immensity of his labors. He was just as courageous the day after defeat as before, and no sooner was a difficulty vanquished, than he sought out and grappled with another. His presence, even, inspired confidence. He had the power of infusing ambition into those around him, and whereever he went there was life and energy. His spirits never seemed to flag like those of other men. He looked a difficulty directly in the face, and walked up to it while looking.

Some men accomplish more in a short life-time, than others in a long one, and so this man, though dead at forty, lived longer and accomplished more than most men do in twice his years. His defects consisted in an over promptness. He seemed so anxious to reach the work that he sometimes went beyond it. Take him for all and all, however, he was a good man, beloved by his family, respected in the community, and an honor to the church of which he was a member. His life and his burial will not soon be forgotten by those among whom he lived. His example shows clearly to all young men that energy and intelligent industry are all that is needed to make farming profitable.

J. N. B.

THE WILL OF JOHN ASHLEY.

Extracts from the Will of John Ashley, dated December 18, 1818, and proved September, 1824. After specifying legacies to his personal friends, he appropriates the residue in the following language: "The pious education of youth, and the diffusion of Christian knowledge among the ignorant and uninformed, and among those whose local circumstances forbid their enjoyment of the stated instructions of the gospel ministry, are objects which now engage the attention of the Christian world, and to the promotion of which, I wish to contribute my mite, with my humble and fervent prayers that the great truths of Christianity may spread and pervade the whole earth, and all may be brought to the knowledge and belief of the truth as it is in Jesus."

For this purpose, he directed his Executors to pay over the residue to a Board of Trustees appointed by him; directing that they apply for an act of incorporation under some appropriate name, and have the power of filling any vacancies in their body.

The Trustees named, were: Heman Day, Ruggles Kent, Jonathan Parsons, Samuel Lathrop and Justin Ely, who were ordered to divide the sum entrusted to them, "into two distinct parts; two-thirds to be appropriated exclusively towards the education of youth within the town of West Springfield, and the remaining one-third to be appropriated towards the propagation and diffusion of Christian knowledge." He directs that the money be placed upon interest, and that portion bequeathed for the spread of the gospel, be equally appropriated for the use of Home Missions, and Foreign Missions. In regard to the distribution of the income of the School Fund, he says: It is my will that no district shall at any time be entitled to, or shall receive any part of the annual dividend, unless their instructor passes the qualifications, and produces the evidence of good moral character by the laws of the Commonwealth, and unless he shall daily make use of the Holy Scriptures as a school book, and shall daily address the Throne of Grace in prayer with his scholars.

If any district shall not be entitled to their dividend according to the rules which I have prescribed, it is my will that the same shall be added to the principal of the fund.

JOHN ASHLEY.

Dr. Sprague, in his Historical Discourse, says: "In the year 1799, Mr. John Ashley, a respectable inhabitant of the parish, offered thirteen hundred pounds, as a fund for the support of the ministry, on condition that the parish would erect a spacious and elegant meeting-house on a spot designated by him, about half a mile from the place where the old meeting-house stood.

"On the sixth of January, 1800, they voted their thankful acceptance of the donation, and thus witnessed the termination of a long and violent contest, which had threatened the dissolution of the society."

In 1792, Mr. Ashley also gave $178.34 to constitute a fund for the support of the communion table of the church.

He gave to the parish a lot of land for a burial-place for the accommodation of the north district of the parish, in 1787, and in 1789, he gave the parish a small library, and in 1819, he gave twenty-two dollars to purchase a Bible for the use of the pulpit.

Mr. Ashley died July 7, 1824, at the age of eighty-five years.

SAMUEL LATHROP, son of Rev. Dr. Joseph Lathrop, was born in 1771, graduated at Yale in 1792, and died in 1846. He studied law; was for ten years a member of the Massachusetts Senate, and President of that body in 1829–30; was a member of Congress from 1818–24; and once ran very close for Governor. He devoted himself considerably to farming in his later years, and contributed much to the improvement of cattle and sheep, potatoes and farm implements in his native town, by purchases and importations.

JERE STEBBINS, who flourished in Ramapogue street, about 1780, was a man of large business capacity. He kept a tavern and store, had a large farm, manufactured earthen ware and saltpetre, and with Moses Day, was extensively engaged in boating on Connecticut river.

Maple Sugar was introduced to the public, by Rev. Samuel Hopkins, second pastor of West Springfield, in a pamphlet published in 1752, giving an account of the Indian way of making it.

Brooms, made from broom corn, were first carried from West Springfield to Boston, by Solomon Todd, who with his own team carried down produce, and brought back goods for Jere Stebbins and others.

Ship-building was once carried on in West Springfield, and the east end of the Common was used as a ship yard.

The schooner "Trial," of sixty tons burthen; the sloop "West Springfield," of about the same calibre, and the sloop "Hampshire," of ninety tons, the latter owned by Samuel Ely and Benjamin Ashley, all were built there and sailed down the river about the year 1800.

MONUMENTAL INSCRIPTIONS AND EPITAPHS.

FROM THE OLD FIRST CEMETERY, CORNER OF CHURCH AND UNION STREETS, BEGUN ABOUT 1700.

Rev. John Woodbridge, first minister of West Springfield, after serving his generation faithfully, fell asleep, June 10, 1718. The righteous will be held in everlasting remembrance. Erected by the descendants of his parishioners, 1852.

Among the first settlers and the earliest families of the town are found the names of Ashley, Bagg, Barber, Bedurtha, Cooper, Day, Dumbleton, Ely, Fowler, Jones, Leonard, Merrick, Miller, Petty, Rogers, Parsons, Smith, Vanhorn and Foster, who gave this ancient burial-ground to the First parish in West Springfield.

Here Rests ye Body of ye Rev^d Mr. Sam^{ll} Hopkins, In whom, sound Judgment, solid Learning, Candour, Piety, Sincerity, Constancy and universal Benevolence combined to form an excellent Minister, a kind Husband, Parent and Friend, who deceased October the 6th, A. D. 1755, in the 62d yr of his age, and 36 year of his ministry.

Mrs. Esther Hopkins, Relict of y^e late Rev^d Mr. Sam^{ll} Hopkins, In whom a superior understanding, uncommon Improvements in Knowledge, exemplary Piety and exalted Virtue combined to form a distinguished female character, $deceas^d$ June 17, 1766, in y^e 72^d year of her age.

FROM THE PAUCATUCK CEMETERY.

BEGUN IN 1770.

In Memory of Mr. Jon^a Smith. The Virtuous Father of a numerous offspring, to whom he gave an example of Piety and Prudence. Who died Feb. 9th, A. D. 1772, In the 75th year of his age.

How blest are they
Who in Christ's bosom sleep.
Cease, then, dear friends,
To mourn, lament or weep.

FROM THE TOWN HOUSE CEMETERY, BEGUN IN 1787.

(The First Burial.)

In memory of Mr. Solomon Lathrop, who, in hope of a blessed immortality, calmly fell asleep April 27, 1787, in the 28th year of his age.

A coffin, sheet and grave is all my earthly store,
'Tis all I want, and kings will have no more.

To the memory of the Rev. Joseph Lathrop, D. D., third pastor of the first church in West Springfield, who died Dec. 31, 1820, aged LXXXIX years and 2 months, and in the LXV year of his ministry.

In memory of Capt. Levi Ely, who was killed Oct. 19, 1786, in the service of his country on the Mohawk river, in the 48th year of his age.

Who dies in youth and vigor dies the best,
Struck thro with wounds, all honest in the breast.

FROM MEETING-HOUSE HILL CEMETERY.

BEGUN IN 1808.

Rev. D. T. Bagg, died Jan. 15, 1848, aged 33. The Pastor, Son and Brother.

Rev. Pliny Butts Day, D. D. Born April 21, 1806, died July 6, 1869. Pastor of Congregational Church, Hollis, N. H.

Rev. Moody Harrington. Died July 22, 1865, aged 67 years. Fervent in spirit, serving the Lord.

FROM THE ASHLEYVILLE CEMETERY.

To the memory of Mr. John Ashley, who died July 17, 1824, Æt 84 years. He was distinguished by Publick Spirit and active benevolence.

THE SOLDIERS' MONUMENT.

IN THE CEMETERY ON MEETING-HOUSE HILL, A BROWN STONE SHAFT, ABOUT TWENTY FEET HIGH, BEARS THE FOLLOWING INSCRIPTIONS:

This Monument is erected in memory of those members of Co. I, 10th Mass. Regiment, who fell in the service of their country, during the Great Rebellion, at Williamsburg, Fair Oaks, Glendale, Malvern, 1st Fredericksburg, Mary's Hights, Salem, 2d Fredericksburg, Gettysburg, Rappahannock Station, Mine Run, Wilderness, Spottsylvania, Coal Harbor, Petersburg.

DIED OF WOUNDS RECEIVED IN ACTION.

Lieut. William Arthur Ashley, May 5, 1864.
Serg't Amos Pettis, Jr., May 3, 1863.
Serg't Osmyn B. Paull, May 18, 1864.
Serg't John R. Walker, August 27, 1864.
Corp'l Hibbard K. Bean, May 31, 1862.
Corp'l James Baldwin, June 13, 1864.
Priv. William H. Estes, May 31, 1862.
Priv. Daniel D. Shea, May 31, 1862.
Priv. Robert J. Stewart, May 31, 1862.
Priv. William H. Atkins, August 12, 1862.
Priv. John Barry, May 3, 1863.
Priv. Hubert J. Boyington, May 3, 1863.
Priv. Anthony Cain, May 15, 1863.
Priv. Charles E. Hovey, May 3, 1863.
Priv. Simeon P. Smith, November 7, 1863.
Priv. Joseph Nugurer, December 10, 1864.
Priv. John E. Casey, May 5, 1864.
Priv. Daniel Cronan, September 19, 1864.

DIED OF DISEASE.

Corp'l Robert Best, Jr., September 2, 1864.
Priv. Jerry Sullivan, September 2, 1861.
Priv. James W. Burr, September 10, 1861.
Priv. John G. Squires, September 13, 1861.
Priv. John Falvey, May 1, 1862.
Priv. Cassander Frisbie, July 12, 1862.
Priv. Charles S. Harris, Jr., September 17, 1862.
Priv. Otis H. Littlejohn, February 5, '63.
Priv. Abner D. Otis, September 16, 1863.

TO THE INTERESTED READER.

THAT many other facts and incidents are worthy of preservation herein, the compiler believes. Those most easy of access within the time specified have been used. To glean, save and deposit in the sacred archives of the town is the privilege and duty of all.

INDEX.

APPENDIX.

www.ingramcontent.com/pod-product-compliance
Lightning Source LLC
LaVergne TN
LVHW021405110826
845150LV00007B/1791

* 9 7 8 1 4 2 5 5 1 2 2 0 0 *